# Kedi

This second book in the Routledge Docalogue series continues to model a new form for the discussion of documentary film, focusing on a new film and a different set of critical questions. *Kedi* (2016) is the first feature documentary by Turkish-American filmmaker Ceyda Torun. The film provides a window into the everyday lives of Istanbul street cats; their itinerant meanderings present a non-human perspective on this ever-changing, ancient city while at the same time exploring the meaningful impact these cats have on the humans they encounter. *Kedi: A Docalogue* brings together a diversity of perspectives on this film. By combining five distinct critical approaches to a single documentary, this book acts both as an intensive scholarly treatment and as a guide for how to analyze, theorize, and contextualize a documentary.

Together, the essays in this book touch upon key topics in documentary studies, including animal studies, eco-documentaries, sound studies, and media industry studies, making them essential reading for scholars interested in contemporary documentary. They also provide useful case studies for teaching documentary film in courses on Contemporary Cinema, Cultural Studies, and Media Industries.

**Jaimie Baron** is an Associate Professor of Film Studies at the University of Alberta. She is the author of two books, *The Archive Effect: Found Footage and the Audiovisual Experience of History* (Routledge, 2014) and *Reuse, Misuse, Abuse: The Ethics of Audiovisual Appropriation in the Digital Era* (2020), and numerous journal articles and book chapters. She is also the director of the Festival of Inappropriation, a yearly international festival of short experimental found footage films and videos.

**Kristen Fuhs** is an Associate Professor of Media Studies at Woodbury University. She writes about documentary film, the American criminal justice system, and contemporary celebrity, and her work has appeared in journals such as *Cultural Studies*; the *Historical Journal of Film, Radio, and Television*; and the *Journal of Sport & Social Issues*.

# Docalogue

Each book in the Docalogue book series highlights a recent documentary film from five different scholarly perspectives. By focusing on a single documentary from multiple points of view, each book demonstrates the ways in which a single film can open onto diverse questions having to do with the status of the "real," documentary ethics, and the politics of representation, among other issues. The book series is an extension of Docalogue.com, a monthly online publication that consists of short essays about contemporary documentary films.

Series Editors: Jaimie Baron and Kristen Fuhs

**I Am Not Your Negro**
A Docalogue
*Edited by Jaimie Baron and Kristen Fuhs*

**Kedi**
A Docalogue
*Edited by Jaimie Baron and Kristen Fuhs*

For more information on the series, visit: https://www.routledge.com/ Docalogue/book-series/DOCALOGUE

# Kedi

## A Docalogue

**Edited by Jaimie Baron and
Kristen Fuhs**

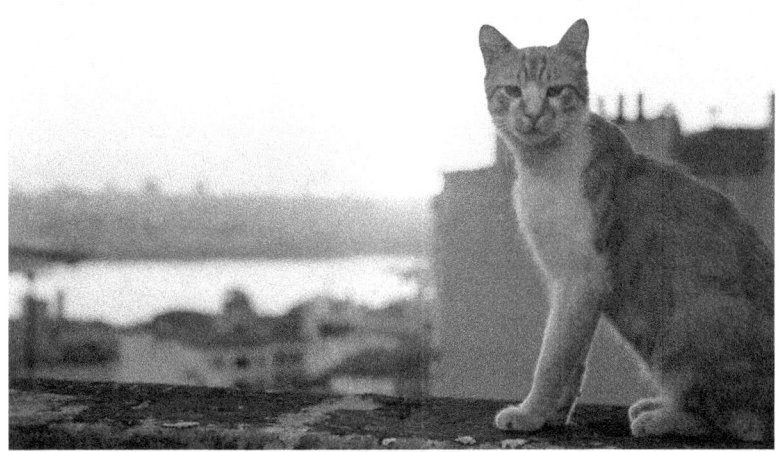

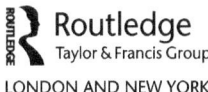 Routledge
Taylor & Francis Group

LONDON AND NEW YORK

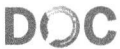

First published 2021
by Routledge
2 Park Square, Milton Park, Abingdon, Oxon OX14 4RN

and by Routledge
52 Vanderbilt Avenue, New York, NY 10017

*Routledge is an imprint of the Taylor & Francis Group, an informa business*

*British Library Cataloguing-in-Publication Data*
A catalogue record for this book is available from the British Library

*Library of Congress Cataloging-in-Publication Data*
Names: Baron, Jaimie, editor. | Fuhs, Kristen, editor.
Title: Kedi : a docalogue / edited by Jaimie Baron and Kristen Fuhs.
Description: Abingdon, Oxon ; New York : Routledge, 2021. | Series: Docalogue; 2 | Includes bibliographical references and index.
Identifiers: LCCN 2020041433 (print) | LCCN 2020041434 (ebook) | ISBN 9780367376116 (hardback) | ISBN 9780429355257 (ebook)
Subjects: LCSH: Kedi (Motion picture)
Classification: LCC PN1997.2.K43 K43 2021 (print) | LCC PN1997.2.K43 (ebook) | DDC 791.43/72--dc23
LC record available at https://lccn.loc.gov/2020041433
LC ebook record available at https://lccn.loc.gov/2020041434

ISBN: 978-0-367-37611-6 (hbk)
ISBN: 978-0-367-70848-1 (pbk)
ISBN: 978-0-429-35525-7 (ebk)

Visit the companion website: www.docalogue.com

Typeset in Bembo
by MPS Limited, Dehradun

# Contents

# List of Illustrations

**Figures**

**Table**

# Preface

Docalogue began in 2017 — and continues — as an online journal, but it also began as a documentary salon in Los Angeles a decade earlier when the editors were both graduate students. Each month, we and a number of friends and colleagues would meet at one of our homes to watch and discuss a documentary film. Although the salon only lasted a year or so, it was one of the most stimulating forums for discussion of documentary film that we experienced during our graduate years. When the editors each moved on to academic jobs in different cities, we continued to meet at conferences, particularly Visible Evidence, which provides a major forum for documentary screening and discussion. Although Visible Evidence is always exciting and generative, we longed to have a way to sustain our discussions of documentary media throughout the year. From this desire arose Docalogue, a digital publication wherein we select one recent documentary each month and solicit two scholars to write a short essay about it, offering two perspectives intended to start off a broader conversation, whether on the website, in classrooms, or within documentary scholarship more broadly.

After about a year of provocative posts in this form, we decided that we might expand the Docalogue format to include short, edited books offering multiple perspectives on a single documentary film — a format that had rarely been tried, at least for nonfiction media. One of the challenges we have faced is how to decide which documentaries to choose as subjects of book-length study. On the website, this is less pressing since we feature so many documentaries, and the purpose is simply to foster scholarly conversation. In choosing documentaries for the book series, however, we are, by definition, singling out particular documentaries that we think have more than passing significance. And, since our focus is recent documentaries, this is necessarily a gamble: we do not know for certain which films will stand the test of time. In addition, while our aim is not to establish a new canon, by virtue of focusing a whole book on a film, we cannot help but raise the profile of the film at least within the documentary scholarly community. In the end, we decided to take the risk and simply choose films that we believe raise important issues about documentary in the contemporary moment and open themselves up to multiple avenues of scholarly analysis. Moreover, our aim is also to center at least some films that emerge from makers whose voices have not always been foregrounded by documentary scholarship.

The purpose of the Docalogue book series is, however, not to close the book, as it were, on any film. The idea is to open up conversation among scholars, to demonstrate to students the many ways of approaching a documentary text, and to offer a resource for those who wish to teach recent documentary films about which little has been written so far. We hope that, like the online journal, the book series will give rise to further scholarship about the films in question.

We would like to thank our Board of Advisors — Chris Cagle, Timothy Corrigan, Oliver Gaycken, Maria Pramaggiore, Pooja Rangan, Mila Turajlić, and Janet Walker — for their advice and suggestions regarding the selection of films and writers. Thanks to Natalie Foster, Sheni Kruger, Jennifer Vennall, and the whole team at Routledge for supporting this series. Our gratitude goes out to all of the writers who have contributed thus far to the Docalogue project — in both the book series and on the website. And a special thanks to Ceyda Torun for the use of her images, and for so graciously taking the time to speak with us about her film!

For more information about the Docalogue website, go to www. docalogue.com.

# Introduction

## *Kedi* in context

*Kristen Fuhs*

Cinema has a deep and abiding fascination with cats. From Edison's *Boxing Cats* (1894) to the ill-fated recent adaptation of the Andrew Lloyd Webber musical *Cats* (Tom Hooper, 2019), the feline figure has long been a subject of intrigue, fancy, and delight on both the big screen and the small. Storied relationships between cats and filmmakers illuminate this connection. Jean Cocteau was president of a club for cat lovers. Chris Marker would send an image of a cat when asked for a portrait of himself. In the wake of her death, tributes to Agnes Varda included both "filmmaker" and "cat-lover" as signifying features in their remembrance. *Kedi*, the 2016 documentary film directed by Ceyda Torun, extends this relationship between cinema, cats, and the filmmakers who love them. Beyond its focus on the many cats who roam the streets of Istanbul, *Kedi* also explores the meaningful impact these cats have on the humans they encounter.

*Kedi: A Docalogue* is the second book in the Docalogue series. We chose *Kedi* for a book-length study because we are interested in what the film's relative commercial success—it was distributed theatrically and earned more than $5 million at the worldwide box office—says about the documentary audience right now and the commercial viability of documentary distribution in the era of streaming video. However, we are also intrigued by the film because of the multiple areas of investigation it opens itself up to, many of which are of particular interest to documentary studies at the moment. The chapters in this volume variously approach the film through lenses related to ecology, animal studies, sound studies, national cinema, and media industries. Together, they demonstrate why a charming film about cats, which was the first feature-length film by its maker, is such a rich text to unpack and analyze.

Chapter 1, Benjamin Schultz-Figueroa's "From cat to clowder: *Kedi* in the anthropocene," looks at *Kedi* through the lens of anthropogenically-induced climate change. The film's representation of cats' proliferation in the urban environment, he argues, is indicative of a broader trend towards representing animals on screen, even as many species have begun to go extinct at unprecedented rates. Schultz-Figueroa draws on theories of ecology and taxidermy to interrogate the ambivalent relationship between preservation and encounter within multispecies documentaries. *Kedi*, he suggests, makes a statement about human/animal relations in the current moment and works as a document of the relationships, fantasies, and desires of a world on the precipice of massive ecological calamity.

Next, Yiman Wang builds on Schultz-Figueroa's interest in the environment and animal studies in "Tracking cats and voicing dogs: locating street animals in *Kedi* and *Taşkafa: stories of the street*" where she compares *Kedi* to *Taşkafa*, another documentary about stray animals in Istanbul. In her comparative analysis, Wang argues that each film differently engages with pressing issues related to the human/non-human relationship as well as the limits of Foucauldian governmentality and environmentality in the Capitalocene. While each film manifests drastically different histories, aesthetics, and sensibilities, Wang suggests they both demonstrate how documentary styles might push against or exceed anthropocentric systems of signification.

In Chapter 3, "Foreign and familiar: *Kedi* and the musicality of Istanbul," Paul Reinsch turns his critical eye to the film's sonic address, arguing that the film creatively uses music to address diverse audiences at different registers. His chapter performs a close analysis of the soundtrack and the score in this documentary, focusing on two specific songs that are emblematic of the film's use of sound to bridge the cultural divide between the East and the West. Reinsch's chapter demonstrates how *Kedi* uses music strategically to stage a series of productive collisions between the foreign and the familiar and between sound and image.

Then, in "*Kedi* between the local and the national," Melis Behlil looks at the film through the lens of national identity, problematizing the concept of a national documentary. Behlil situates *Kedi* as part of a long history of documentaries about Turkey, many of which were made by outsiders. Although set entirely in Istanbul and shot in the Turkish language, most of the main crew (including the Turkish-born director) are based in the US. Rather than Turkish or American, Behlil suggests *Kedi* might be thought of as an "Istanbullu" film, one whose local signifiers are aligned closely with the city, but which sidesteps any clear identification with national culture.

In Chapter 5, "*Kedi*: crossover documentary as popular art cinema" Chris Cagle takes a media industries approach to the film, examining it in relation to other 2017 documentaries and suggesting a relationship between distribution tiers and different taste categories. Cagle proposes four broad categories for thinking through the relationship between documentary style and industrial hierarchy: the popular documentary, the crossover documentary, the mainstay documentary, and the cinephile documentary. By looking at *Kedi* as an example of a crossover documentary—something that is not quite popular documentary, but not quite art cinema—he argues that this in-between quality suggests something about commerce, identity, and documentary aesthetics in the contemporary mediascape.

Finally, the collection ends with a conversation with *Kedi*'s director, Ceyda Torun, which touches on, and in many ways responds to, the critical threads that are woven throughout this collection. By putting Torun into conversation with the different chapters in this book, we hope to reinforce the goals of the Docalogue project—to open up new avenues of inquiry about this film while engaging in a robust dialogue about contemporary documentary more broadly. As one of the humans in *Kedi* says, "having a relationship with cats must be a lot like being friends with aliens. You make contact with a very different life form, open a line of communication with one another, and start a dialogue." Whether such dialogue takes place between humans, animals, or alien beings, we can only hope this book will continue to spark the discussion.

# 1 From cat to clowder

## *Kedi* in the anthropocene

*Benjamin Schultz-Figueroa*

There are two crucial, yet divergent, moments in Ceyda Torun's 2016 documentary *Kedi*, which seem to speak to each other from across the film. The first occurs early on when a fishmonger describes his relationship with a cat who frequently comes to his store. "It's fascinating," he says, "they're just like people." The audience views the cat up close as it peers over the shop's roof, is fed by one of the shopkeepers, and plays with its food. Then, we watch one of the shop employees shaking a bucket of sardines out onto the street. The cat gingerly approaches and picks at the sardines but is quickly overwhelmed by an oncoming flock of seagulls that descend *en masse* to devour the fish. The cat slinks away from the ensuing feeding frenzy, its silky form a stark contrast to the audiovisual cacophony of the shrieking and flapping gulls (Figure 1.1). As is typical of *Kedi*, which takes great pains to depict cats as emotive, complex onscreen characters, it seems to exude disdain for the squawking birds desperately fighting over the bounty of fish, evoking a sense of pride that distinguishes the cat from the mass of less charismatic seagulls. This scene is later darkly reflected in a sequence that comes towards the end of the film. A man carrying a bag of fish parts wanders through the city, feeding the many stray cats of Istanbul. He approaches a small weatherworn dock. There, a cat spots him, meows, and suddenly ten other cats leap out from underneath the dock to surround the man and eat the food he presents them. This dynamic is repeated in scene after scene, where the man is met by different groups of cats around the city who suddenly congregate for his handouts. Weaving underfoot, their meowing overlapping on the soundtrack, these felines who have been meticulously individuated throughout the rest of the film become anonymous members of a clowder, or group of cats. They are now like the seagulls at the beginning of the film, a mass of hungry, desperate animals.

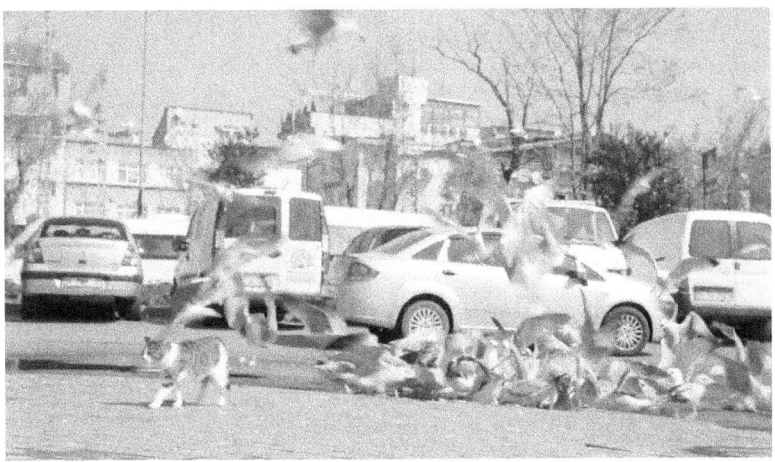

*Figure 1.1* Seagulls swarm for food while a cat slinks away in *Kedi* (Ceyda Torun, 2016).

This chapter considers *Kedi*'s fluid representation of felines as symptomatic of broader shifts in human/animal relationships in contemporary life. John Berger famously argued that as animals began to disappear from daily life throughout the 19th century, representations of them multiplied to make up for their absence.[1] Akira Lippit further elaborates that the invention of film accelerated this process, rapidly transferring animal life from living bodies to onscreen images.[2] I claim here that we are living through a similar moment now. As species go extinct at unprecedented rates, large portions of animal life are no longer just disappearing from urban and suburban locales but threatening to vanish from the planet itself. And yet, their images multiply onscreen as never before. In the last ten years, an explosion of internationally acclaimed animal documentaries has been released, including Illisa Barbash and Lucian Castaing-Taylor's *Sweetgrass* (2009), Nicolas Philbert's *Nénette* (2010), Castaing-Taylor and Verena Paravel's *Leviathan* (2012), and Denis Côté's *Bestiaire* (2012). Unlike the overdetermined structures of *National Geographic* or *Planet Earth* documentaries, these films are deeply invested in animals as contingent and aberrant documentary subjects that confound anthropomorphic descriptions and meaning-making. Driven by a growing concern over climate change as well as scholarly and artistic interest in multispecies ethnography and ecocinema, these films use new visualizing methods and technologies to depict their animals as opaque and fascinating subjects. Here, I position *Kedi*—with its polyvocal representations of cats as subjects of capitalist power, symbols of ahistorical nature, alien beings outside human history, and mirrors for humanity—within this frenzy to capture animal specificity and complexity in an era of ecological collapse.

This chapter is divided into two sections. Practicing what Jennifer Peterson and Graig Alan Uhlin describe as the reverse-zoom method for studying Anthropocene history, each section operates on a different scale.[3] The first section zooms out, considering the ambivalent relationship between preservation and encounter within the broader movement of multispecies documentaries in ecocinema discourse. Despite individually attracting a fair amount of critical attention, these multispecies documentaries have yet to be extensively considered as a historical genre. Doing so reveals patterns in their aesthetics, programs, and receptions that might otherwise be invisible and raises questions about how the films will persist and be understood beyond this particular moment in time. Unlike much of the scholarly writing about these films, which focuses on a framework of encounter and liveliness, this first section proposes the lens of taxidermy to explain their persistent elements of mourning and loss. The second section zooms in on *Kedi*'s own articulation of these themes, putting the analytical lens of taxidermy to use. Using ecological studies to recontextualize moments in the film, it compares *Kedi* to other strains of discourse surrounding stray cats in Istanbul. I conclude that *Kedi* functions less as a holistic statement about human/animal relations than as a document of the incommensurable anxieties, fantasies, and desires of a world on the precipice of massive ecological calamity.

## Zoom out: ecocinema, multispecies documentaries, and loss

The July 1975 edition of *Bioscience*, a peer-reviewed journal put out by the American Institute of Biological Sciences, contains a one-page entry titled "Ecocinema: A Plan for Preserving Nature."[4] Originally written in 1966 by Roger C. Anderson for his university newspaper, this brief essay responds to the ongoing public debates surrounding pollution and deforestation, which led to the eventual establishment and reinforcement of the Environmental Protection Agency in the 1960s and 1970s. Written as a satire, Anderson offers a facetious solution to the problems of degraded natural environments and species loss. In addition to the wide-scale preservation of animals in formaldehyde, he proposes: "I would have motion pictures taken of all-natural communities with close-up sequences of individual plants and animals in them." He goes on to describe how these films would then be screened in special theaters created to saturate the viewers' senses, including not only audio and images but also manufactured scents to reproduce the smells of flowers, treadmills to amplify spectators' sense of movement, climate control to mimic different atmospheres, a variety of props to simulate streams and leaves underfoot, and an electronically produced echo system that would carry viewers voices back to them. The goal would be to reproduce the experience of nature in all its particulars, immersive down to the last detail. This new media form would quell the concerns of even the most ardent nature lovers while permitting urbanization and industry to progress without worry. Anderson concludes his biting satire by claiming that it would allow humanity to "proceed to make a pestiferous nature a habitat fit for creation's most noble animal." His title for this fictional method of preservation is "ecocinema."[5]

Within the context of film studies, the term "ecocinema" no longer carries such associations even as the issues that drove Anderson—persistent deforestation, rising extinction rates, and anthropogenic effects on climate—have all ratcheted up exponentially. Ecocinema is an amorphous and contested term that describes works that varyingly portray ecological subject matters, connect viewers more deeply with natural phenomena, advocate environmental activism, or embody a materialist ecological approach to filming. Some essential texts in this scholarly debate include David Ingram's *Green Screen: Environmentalism and Hollywood Cinema*, which studies the environmental politics of nature in Hollywood films; Scott MacDonald's *The Garden in the Machine*, which posits experimental landscape films as an outgrowth of American nature painting; and the anthology *Ecocinema Theory and Practice*, which works to expand the definition of ecocinema as a framework for analyzing the ecological impact of nearly any film.[6] From these various vantage points, ecocinema scholarship works to position the moving image as a crucial node in the multifaceted relationship between nature and culture and as a means of expanding human attention and care to natural phenomena

A central topic in this conversation is the cinematic depiction of animals. Throughout film history, animals have been subjects of fascination and prime attractions for movie-going audiences.[7] From the earliest safari travelogues to the most recent PBS wildlife series, filmmakers have used animal images to navigate differing relationships with the environment, embodying ideologically-charged notions such as "the circle of life" or "survival of the fittest" in their depictions.[8] In our current era of climate change, new articulations of this relationship have emerged in a group of animal documentaries that define themselves against the tropes of past animal films, especially the infantilizing anthropomorphism of those produced by Disney. These films have their roots in posthumanist scholarship and the anthropological fieldwork practices that Eben Kirksey and Stefan Helmreich call "multispecies ethnography."[9] Faye Ginsburg identifies Illisa Barbash and Lucien Castaing-Taylor's 2009 film *Sweetgrass* as an inaugural work for the genre, which established the shared goal of operating "beyond the discursive and the anthropocentric."[10] In addition to *Sweetgrass*, other prominent examples include those listed in the introduction: *Nénette*, *Leviathan*, *Bestiaire*, and *Kedi*. Academics and critics alike have praised multispecies documentaries for reasserting the alienness of animals as onscreen subjects, who do not have transparent motivations or plotlines that recognizably mirror our own. These commentators often focus on the indexical capacities of the moving image apparatus, which the filmmakers use to capture or simulate nonhuman experiences through cameras attached to animals, extensive use of long-takes, or camera movements that approximate nonhuman points of view. Cumulatively, this critical response describes film and video as creating portals into the sensory experiences of a non-narrative, nonhuman, natural world. As Laura McMahon and Michael Lawrence write of *Nénette*, such films are thought to display "a particular attentiveness to animal life that opens to more fluid, dynamic modes of cross-species relationality."[11] By breaking out of the narrative strictures guiding past animal representations and innovatively immersing viewers in the lives of animals, these multispecies documentaries are archetypal examples of ecocinema's entryway into the world beyond the human.

The interest in ecocinema and multispecies documentary as immersive encounters with nonhuman nature leads back to Anderson's original concerns when coining the term "ecocinema." Chris Tong suggests that one might even read contemporary ecocinema scholarship as sincerely pursuing what Anderson sarcastically proposed in the 1960s.[12] There are certainly some striking overlaps. In Scott MacDonald's foundational 2004 essay "Toward an Eco-Cinema," he mirrors Anderson when he writes: "If we cannot halt the decay and transformation of the natural world or of cinema, we can certainly honor those dimensions of what is disappearing around us that we *would* preserve if we could, and we can hope that by valuing what seems on the verge of utter demise, we can hold onto it longer than may seem possible."[13] Here, as in Anderson's writing, ecocinema supplies a means of preservation in the face of extinction and habitat destruction. Inevitable disappearance is a common theme in these films. Multispecies documentarians often choose to train their cameras on vanishing animals, threatened environments, or rapidly changing human/nature relationships, such as *Sweetgrass'* depiction of Montana's last sheepherders, *Leviathan's* focus on the dying fishing industry in New Bedford, Massachusetts, *Nénette's* depiction of an aging orangutan at the end of her life in the Jardin des Plantes in Paris, or *Kedi's* threatened community of stray cats and the people who love them. Key to so many of these films is the desire to honor and preserve what is thought to be disappearing before it is gone, suggesting a deep melancholy and ambivalent core to ecocinema alongside its lively engagement with other forms of life. Despite using a theoretical framework of encounter and relational becoming, many of these films also function as monuments, artifacts, tombs, heirlooms, or specimen jars.

In both MacDonald's and Anderson's descriptions of ecocinema, we see reflections of what Fatimah Tobing Rony describes as the taxidermist impulse in ethnographic film, which she defines, following Haraway, as "a means to protect against loss, in order that the body may be transcended."[14] Rony chronicles how early ethnographers assumed the inevitable disappearance of their subjects, leading to a desire to save detailed recordings of "vanishing" habitats, people, and cultures for the sake of posterity. These films were contrived as timeless images of seemingly direct encounters, which were meant to be repeated long after the death and disappearance of their profilmic subjects. Despite their many differences, contemporary multispecies documentaries share this common anticipation of a loss yet-to-come with early ethnography. Both sets of films work to create what Rony calls the "cinematic ethnographic present," where that which is thought to be disappearing continues to exist in the experience of the spectators watching the film.[15] The construction of multispecies documentaries as immersive unfolding engagements with living beings is a crucial component in this process of salvaging the present, wherein the immediacy of the viewer's experience contrasts with the inevitable loss of the profilmic subjects. These films address the spectator in the always-active present tense, existing beyond the degrading effects of history and habitat destruction by presenting us with experiences that can be relived endlessly in the future.

Within the context of climate change, the taxidermic function of multispecies documentaries might best be seen as an extension of current anxieties about the future. Even as these documentaries never depict the future itself, they create variations on what E. Ann Kaplan calls "memory for the future."[16] Kaplan uses the term to describe how science fiction films allow contemporary audiences to process the destructive effects of climate change by generating possible memories of what might come.

These manufactured memories become a part of how we think through our uncertain future. Multispecies documentaries engage audiences in a similar dynamic. Here, we watch both as viewers in the present and as possible viewers from a future when the onscreen animals are gone. Our fascination with the details of these animals—with all of the alien particulars of their bodies, behavior, and senses—is informed by our knowledge of their threatened disappearance. Projecting a world to come where these films are all that is left of their subjects, we watch them as a form of mourning for what is not-yet-lost and as a means of speculatively trying on our own future perspectives.

None of this refutes the importance of these films as engagements with a nonhuman material world. It is, of course, possible that multispecies documentaries can be both encounters and specimens, expanding the human sensorium while simultaneously creating an anticipatory nostalgia for lifeforms soon to be extinct. Rather than as an either/or proposition, it is perhaps best to consider these as two drives that pull contemporary animal documentaries in their own directions. Specific films navigate these desires in distinct ways, producing meaningful differences in their relationship to the onscreen animal subjects and our collective future. Focusing on both of these drives within the multispecies documentary may temper our tendency to produce organicist readings of them, in which the film itself is treated as a living whole.[17] Instead of considering multispecies documentaries as holistic experiences of phenomena outside the human, we might pay more attention to the stitching and craftwork that constitutes the genre. There lie consequential differences between and within these films in the workings of their images and the craft of their production. As Michael Metzger writes of *Leviathan*, "[t]he fluidity of its mobile gaze and its hidden splices belie incommensurable contradictions."[18] Viewing multispecies documentaries as taxidermic specimens entail picking at the threads holding these contradictions together, undoing their seams, revealing new meanings in the leftover skeins of skin and scraps of stuffing.

## Zoom in: from cats to clowders

The term for a group of cats, "clowder," was originally a variation of "clutter," meaning a "crowd, heap, or cluster."[19] Clowder's etymology brings with it the ignoble history of the cat, which was long considered a pest before it was a pet. As Katharine Rogers describes, cats were "the last of the familiar domestic animals to be domesticated" and have often been treated cruelly or sadistically throughout human history.[20] As a word, clowder-as-clutter asks to be cleaned up, swept away, or otherwise disposed of, evoking a confusing mass, turmoil, or clotted lump. The tension between the charismatic, companionable, individual cat, and the more unsavory clutter of the clowder is central to *Kedi*. The film's documented difference between how Istanbul's city planners see cats—as an impediment to health and progress—and *Kedi*'s human interviewees describe them—conveying deeply personal relationships with individual cats—rests on this division between viewing cats as a statistical mass or as charismatic individuals.

The Turkish government has a long history of treating cats, as well as stray dogs, as problems to be eradicated. As Didem Tali describes for the *New York Times*, citrinin poison was used to painfully exterminate large numbers of stray animals throughout the country in the late 1990s and early 2000s.[21] Strays pose real and tangible threats, as Tali describes, including the spread of rabies and other diseases through bites and fecal matter. Popular resistance to these practices in Turkey shifted most of the extermination programs to a catch, spay, neuter, and release procedure. Still, concerns about overpopulation persist, and culling remains an option. In 2016, the same year that *Kedi* was released, Istanbul's Chamber of Veterinary Surgeons raised an alarm over the ballooning population of strays in the city, which they estimated included over 700,000 cats.[22] These government agencies, politicians, and veterinary doctors, discuss the issue of stray cats at a scale that dramatically reframes the human/animal relationship away from the individual cat and towards the cat-as-clowder, a controversial move that has been historically contested in Turkey.

*Kedi* and its filmmakers are clearly partisan participants in these debates. In an interview with *TRT World*, Torun recognizes the "concern over representing the darker side of cats' lives in Istanbul" but stipulates that the film was meant to focus on the generosity of humans in the face of these worries about feline overpopulation.[23] *Kedi*'s press-kit and website emphasize the cats' individual characters by profiling seven of them. Each profile includes a description of appearance, gender, "profession," location, and nicknames, such as "San—The Hustler" and "Bengü—The Lover." Onscreen, the film individuates the cats primarily through voiceover, where humans describe their beloved companions over corroborating images. These descriptions alternate between cats as alien life forms, God-sent messengers, industrious workers, street brawlers, carefree tramps, and pampered aristocrats. At times, *Kedi* leverages the communal relationships between individual cats and humans into a utopian vision, evoking a network of self-organized mutual aid beyond official government programs. The film suggests that Istanbul's sapien and feline residents fundamentally rely on each other for emotional and material care in several touching moments. Graig Uhlin notes that in *Kedi,* cats take on surprising political significance as subtle figures of defiance.[24] He points to popular resistance to President Recep Tayyip Erdoğan's 2012 attempts to exterminate and curtail strays as a moment of shared political struggle between the two species. Like in Chris Marker's *The Grin Without a Cat* (1977) and *The Case of the Grinning Cat* (2004), the fickle cats of *Kedi* are associated with political dissidents, emblemized by the image of a lone stray in front of anti-Erdoğan graffiti declaring: "ERDO-GONE!" The film summarizes these notions of political resistance through a penultimate montage of urban development paired with the audio of interviewees lamenting the city's changing landscape and vanishing regard for strays. As one speaker states "If you ask me, the trouble street cats or other street animals face are not independent from the troubles we all face." These troubles may remain largely undefined by the film, but they do evoke a looming threat that suggests a shared political project facing Istanbul's multi-species inhabitants.

The image of the politically resistant feline is mirrored by its resistance as a cinematic subject. Theorizing cats' onscreen presence in film history, Rosalind Galt highlights their insistent independence, describing them as avatars for "the exhilaration of a cinematic life not quite under human control."[25] Many of *Kedi*'s delights come from this very aspect, watching the lithe cats unpredictably make their way through Istanbul's back-streets, roofs, and squares. *Kedi* was specially constructed to create these experiences. As they emphasize in the press-kit, director Ceyda Torun and cinematographer Charlie Wuppermann adapted their equipment and shooting style in an effort to "capture the essence of what it means to be a cat in Istanbul."[26] Through the use of drones, Steadicams, and close-ups, the film presents the cats in a variety of dynamic vignettes that heighten their visual fascination. Extreme close-ups on cat faces focus audiences on their inscrutable microexpressions and beautifully strange physiognomy. As Yiman Wang observes, much of *Kedi*'s camerawork and editing mobilizes the tropes of the city symphony to picture a cat's eye view of Istanbul, using "the slinking cats' erratic footwork to reframe human pedestrians and the built environment from the feline perspective."[27] Like film itself, cats provide a vantage point for viewers to experience otherwise unseen and underground realities of the city.

These elements constitute the overriding direction of *Kedi,* where cats are regal and privileged cinematic subjects whose tangled relationships with humans in Istanbul are honored. Scenes of human/animal bonding are dynamically stitched together to create an affirmative vision of the multispecies community in the face of major institutional obstacles.

However, when considered a work of taxidermy, there are dangling threads in the film's seams that can be tugged at, in a cat-like gesture, and which unravel into terrains beyond its primary focus. *Kedi*'s images of a shifting ecosystem evoke a darker, off-screen tale of urban development in a time of climate change and species eradication, which can only be illuminated with further context. Following Uhlin, it is important to consider the ecological role of cats as synanthropes (human adjacent animals) within the urban habitat of Istanbul.[28] While urban growth threatens many species with extinction, it generally leads to growing, rather than shrinking, cat populations. As Michael McKinney describes in the journal *Biological Conservation*, urbanization's main effect on variegated habitats is the destruction of native species and its replacement with a homogenized set of human-adjacent animals.[29] McKinney writes that as urban environments are built to sustain human life, synanthropes like cats are "not only able to colonize cities but they can attain population densities far above those found under natural conditions."[30] Viewed from the perspective of biological conservation, cats—like rats, seagulls, raccoons, and others—are often the vanguard of the city's homogenizing effects on local environments, growing in numbers to fill the empty holes that humans punch into ecological systems.

An against-the-grain reading of *Kedi* focusing on this ecological impact would change the register of many of the film's scenes. The film's meticulously created cats-eye-view camera can be considered a variation on other cat-cameras, such as those produced by The National Geographic & University of Georgia's *Kitty Cam Project*. Here, recordings were made by attaching small cameras to urban housecats in order to study their behavioral patterns. These videos stand in stark contrast to *Kedi*'s gliding low angle camera. The kitty cam videos are ungainly, their soundtracks consisting of insulated jostling noises that evoke the material presence of the camera as it unceremoniously swings around the necks of the cats going about their daily routines. The images jerk back and forth, often disturbingly off-kilter, as the cats drag the viewer along. As Donna Haraway describes the genre of unedited crittercam videos, these are "more like an acid trip than a peephole to reality."[31] Lacking the human voiceover and the Steadicam's stabilizing mechanisms, which define the POV shots in *Kedi*, these images are profoundly disorienting and alienating. Crucially, the meaning derived from these films is also very different than those in *Kedi*. As many news reports pointed out, the main takeaway from the *Kitty Cam Project* was the astonishing scope of feline predation on other species.[32] Dr. George Fenwick, President of American Bird Conservancy, responded to the published findings of these experiments by writing that cats in the United States alone are "likely killing more than 4 billion animals per year."[33] Stripped of the human relationships that defined the cats in *Kedi* and placed within the context of ecological conservation, the kitty cam videos point to cats' role in furthering destructive anthropogenic effects on habitats and ecosystems. Studies such as these have been used to advocate for the mass extermination of large percentages of the cat population.[34]

Homogenizing habitats through urban growth and the corresponding inflation in numbers of particular species is as essential a part of the story of global climate change as the disappearance of other species. Some animals, which were once contained within local ecologies, are going to experience monstrous population growths. As Anna Tsing, Heather Swanson, Elaine Gan, and Nils Bubandt write in *Arts of Living on a Damaged Planet*: "Monsters are useful figures with which to think the Anthropocene, this time of massive human transformations of multi-species life and their uneven effects."[35] Although *Kedi*'s structure does not encourage this reading, the cats in the film could be viewed as adorable iterations of such monsters. They might be compared to the monstrous synanthropes from other multispecies documentaries, such as the seagulls in *Leviathan* or the rats in *Rat Film* (Theo Anthony, 2016). Like the animals in these other films, the cats often clutter the screen in *Kedi*. Their repeated presence and accumulated images obliquely reflect their broader proliferation just off-screen, where the individual animals we follow in the film get lost in the clowder of feral cats prowling the city streets (Figure 1.2). The importance of *Kedi*'s reliance on the

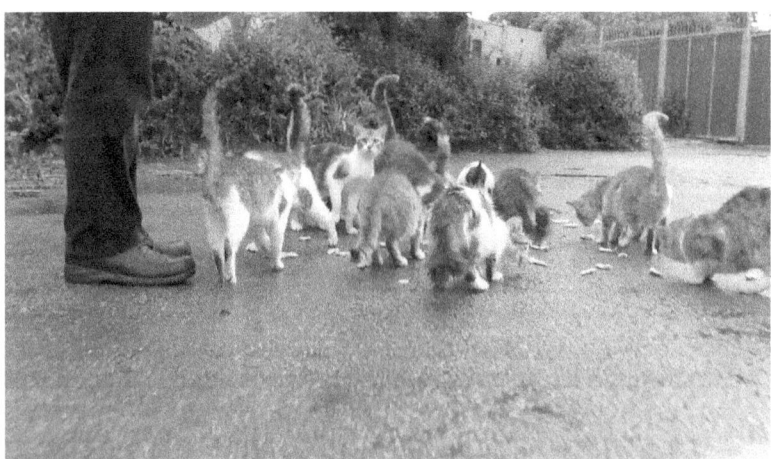

*Figure 1.2* A clowder of cats congregates to be fed in *Kedi* (Ceyda Torun, 2016).

Steadicam's stabilizing mechanism ultimately distinguishes its cats from the disorienting depictions of other synanthropes. Like the film itself, the Steadicam struggles to provide stability and order in unstable surroundings while creating a sense of soothing, smooth, forward movement even amongst the bustle and confusion of the city streets. The steadying structure of these shots and the film itself palliate our potential concerns over what might otherwise be monstrous images.

The tension between cats as individual pets and clowders as monstrous populations is a defining tension in the film and in our historical moment. As the effects of climate change are becoming more and more apparent, human futures are correspondingly becoming more and more tied up with animal wellbeing. Changes in animal lives both directly impact and metaphorically reflect changes in our own. Where they go, we follow. Perhaps the most dramatic example of this in a lifetime is currently unfolding (as of this writing) in the COVID-19 epidemic, where a zoonotic virus has tied the fate of millions of people to the effects of biodiversity and habitat destruction.[36] Under these circumstances, we should all be looking more intently at animals as many of them disappear, and other populations grow to monstrous proportions. Given the intractable realities of climate change and the hazards awaiting us in this new era, *Kedi* prompts the question of how we plan to retain human/animal communities like the one it documents. The dreams of mutual assistance presented by the film's human testimonials stand in stark contrast to the brutal circumstances projected by today's best climate models. Whether spectators will continue to view *Kedi*'s cats as they are intended to be seen by the filmmakers—as fascinating, emotive, charismatic individuals—or watch them with the sense of awe and dread evoked by the seagulls in *Leviathan* will largely be determined by events yet to come. The roles of animals in cities, especially coastal megacities like Istanbul, will be radically reshaped as rising seawaters, climbing temperatures, ever more frequent catastrophic storms, and increasing climate-driven inequality transform urban centers.[37] Generally, as a genre, multispecies documentary invites us to anticipate these new, difficult futures just around the corner. In their open-ended structures and intense interest in nonhuman life, these films usher us onto a new terrain, where our relationships with animals might be unrecognizably altered, even including our enduring love of cats. As an entry into this genre, *Kedi* attempts to construct a stable craft for the rough seas ahead, a space where human/feline love can be preserved despite the crushing pressures which will, inevitably, be placed on this relationship. The film suggests we should think deeply about how we plan to confront these issues, as our treatment of the cats going forward may reflect upon us in profound ways. As one of *Kedi*'s interviewees concludes: "It would be easy to see street cats as a problem and handle them as a problem. Whereas if we can learn to live together again, maybe we'll solve our own problems as we try to solve theirs."

## Notes

1 John Berger, *About Looking* (New York: Pantheon Books, 1980), 15.
2 Akira Mizuta Lippit, *Electric Animal: Toward a Rhetoric of Wildlife* (Minneapolis: University of Minnesota Press, 2000), 184–185.
3 Jennifer Peterson and Graig Uhlin, "In Focus: Film and Media Studies in the Anthropocene," *JCMS: Journal of Cinema & Media Studies* 58, no. 2 (2019): 145.
4 Roger C. Anderson, "Reflections: Ecocinema: A Plan for Preserving Nature," *BioScience* 25, no. 7 (1975): 452.
5 Aldo Leopold, *A Sand County Almanac & Other Writings on Ecology and Conservation*, Special commemorative ed., Library of America 238 (New York: Library of America, 2013). This past summer, I wrote to Dr. Anderson, now an Emeritus Distinguished University Professor of Ecology at Illinois State University, to ask him to contextualize his writing from over 50 years ago. He responded by citing Aldo Leopold's classic work of ecological literature *A Sand County Almanac: And Sketches Here and There* as an inspiration for his essay. Anderson wrote: "In the first two sentences of the foreword to Sand County Almanac, Leopold wrote that 'There are some who can live without wild things, and some who cannot. These essays are delights and dilemmas of one who cannot.' People who do not have a connection with nature and have little or no interest in preserving nature are defined in Ecocinema." For Anderson, following Leopold, recording moving images of nature was aligned with the processes destroying that very nature, greasing the wheels for its destruction by palliating the loss that such destruction causes. Here, he picks up on a longstanding critique of the moving image in ecological writing. Indeed, just a few sentences after those cited by Anderson, Leopold observes that, for the nature lover, "the opportunity to see geese is more important than television." For naturalists like Anderson and Leopold, the immersive effects of film and TV are viewed with suspicion as part and parcel with humanity's domination of its habitat and extradition from nature.
6 See David Ingram, *Green Screen: Environmentalism and Hollywood Cinema* (Exeter: University of Exeter Press, 2004); Scott MacDonald, *The Garden in the Machine a Field Guide to Independent Films about Place* (Berkeley: University of California Press, 2001); Paula Willoquet-Maricondi, *Framing the World: Explorations in Ecocriticism and Film* (Charlottesville: University of Virginia Press, 2010); and Stephen Rust, Salma Monani, and Sean Cubitt, *Ecocinema Theory and Practice* (Hoboken: Taylor and Francis, 2012).
7 Scholars such as Cynthia Chris, Derek Bousé, and Gregg Mitman have all chronicled the contested nature of animal documentaries. See Cynthia Chris, *Watching Wildlife* (Minneapolis: University of Minnesota Press, 2006); Derek Bousé, *Wildlife Films* (Philadelphia: University of Pennsylvania Press, 2000); Gregg Mitman, *Reel Nature: America's Romance with Wildlife on Film* (Cambridge, MA: Harvard University Press, 1999).
8 Ingram, *Green Screen: Environmentalism and Hollywood Cinema*, 69–71.

9 S. Eben Kirksey and Stefan Helmreich, "The Emergence of Multispecies Ethnography," *Cultural Anthropology* 25, no. 4 (2010): 545–76.

10 Faye Ginsburg, "Decolonizing Documentary On-Screen and Off: Sensory Ethnography and the Aesthetics of Accountability," *Film Quarterly* 72, no. 1 (2018): 41.

11 Michael Lawrence and Laura McMahon, eds., *Animal Life and the Moving Image* (London; New York: Palgrave, on behalf of the British Film Institute, 2015), 5.

12 Chris Tong, "Ecocinema for All: Reassembling the Audience," *Interactions: Studies in Communication & Culture* 4, no. 2 (October 1, 2013): 115.

13 Scott MacDonald, "Toward an Eco-Cinema," *Interdisciplinary Studies in Literature and Environment* 11, no. 2 (2004): 108.

14 Fatimah Tobing Rony, *The Third Eye: Race, Cinema, and Ethnographic Spectacle* (Durham, NC: Duke University Press, 1996), 102.

15 Despite the human emphasis of the "ethno" in ethnography, Rony's description of taxidermy clearly includes nonhuman animals as subjects of the ethnographic eye. Rony, 102.

16 E. Ann Kaplan, *Climate Trauma: Foreseeing the Future in Dystopian Film and Fiction* (New Brunswick, NJ: Rutgers University Press, 2016), 4.

17 For an example of this type of holism, see Lucien Castaing-Taylor's claim that the long takes "reflect an ambiguity of meaning that is at the heart of human experience itself." Here, evoking Bergson's writing on film, the long take's unfolding in time creates a synthesized experience beyond the construct of the cinematic apparatus. Lucien Castaing-Taylor, "Iconophobia," *Transition* 6, no. 69 (1996): 76.

18 Michael Metzger, "Leviathan's Labors Lost, Or: Who Works After The Subject?" *Millennium Film Journal* 61 (Spring 2015): 38.

19 "cludder, n." OED Online. Oxford University Press, September 2019, accessed October 24, 2019, https://www-oed-com.oca.ucsc.edu/view/Entry/34828?rskey=2Pgo70&result=1&isAdvanced=false.

20 Katharine M. Rogers, *Cat* (London: Reaktion Books, 2006), 9.

21 Didem Tali, "A New Deal for Turkey's Homeless Dogs: Fixes," *The New York Times*, October 2, 2019.

22 Anadolu Agency, "Battle to Care for Istanbul's Stray Animals Continues," *Hurriyet Daily News,* April 18, 2016. http://www.hurriyetdailynews.com/battle-to-care-for-istanbuls-stray-animals-continues-97951.

23 Melis Alemdar, "Hit Film About Istanbul's Cats Finally Comes Home to Turkey," *TRT World,* June 1, 2017. https://www.trtworld.com/magazine/hit-film-about-istanbul-s-cats-finally-comes-home-to-turkey-7498.

24 Graig Uhlin, "On Street Cats and City Rats: Synanthropes and Cinematic Ecologies," *The Cine-Files* 14 (Spring 2019), http://www.thecine-files.com/uhlin/.

25 Rosalind Galt, "Cats and the Moving Image: Feline Cinematicity from Lumiere to Maru," in *Animal Life and the Moving Image*, eds. Michael Lawrence and Laura McMahon (London; New York: Palgrave, on behalf of the British Film Institute, 2015), 44.

26 "KEDi Press Kit," accessed December 30, 2019, https://www.dropbox.com/sh/5vyuub2vr764uc7/AABV1NpXd-sfTYz3qEWRFx0da?dl=0.

27 Yiman Wang, "A Feline City Symphony," *Docalogue,* May 2018, https://docalogue.com/may-kedi/.

28 Uhlin, "On Street Cats and City Rats."

29 Michael L. McKinney, "Urbanization as a Major Cause of Biotic Homogenization," *Biological Conservation* 127, no. 3 (January 2006): 247–60.

30 McKinney, 249.

31 Donna J. Haraway, "Crittercam: Compounding Eyes in Naturecultures," in *When Species Meet* (Minneapolis: University of Minnesota Press, 2008), 258.

32 Slate Video Staff, "Kitty Cam: The Project Attaching Cameras to Cats as They Move through the Wild," accessed December 30, 2019, https://slate.com/news-and-politics/2012/08/kitty-cam-the-project-attaching-cameras-to-cats-as-they-move-through-the-wild.html.

33 American Bird Conservancy, "'KittyCam' Reveals High Levels of Wildlife Being Killed by Outdoor Cats," accessed December 30, 2019, https://abcbirds.org/article/kittycam-reveals-high-levels-of-wildlife-being-killed-by-outdoor-cats/.

34 Peter P. Marra, *Cat Wars: The Devastating Consequences of a Cuddly Killer* (Princeton: University Press, 2016), 63.

35 Anna Lowenhaupt Tsing et al., *Arts of Living on a Damaged Planet. Ghosts of the Anthropocene; Monsters of the Anthropocene* (Minneapolis: University of Minnesota Press, 2017), M2.

36 John Vidal, "'Tip of the Iceberg': Is Our Destruction of Nature Responsible for Covid-19?" *The Guardian*, March 18, 2020, https://www.theguardian.com/environment/2020/mar/18/tip-of-the-iceberg-is-our-destruction-of-nature-responsible-for-covid-19-aoe.

37 For a breakdown of climate change's effects on Istanbul, see: Hüseyin Toros, Mohsen Abbasnia, Mustafa Sagdic, and Mete Tayanç, "Long-Term Variations of Temperature and Precipitation in the Megacity of Istanbul for the Development of Adaptation Strategies to Climate Change," *Advances in Meteorology* (2017), https://doi.org/10.1155/2017/6519856; Fatih Kara and Ismail Yucel, "Climate Change Effects on Extreme Flows of Water Supply Area in Istanbul: Utility of Regional Climate Models and Downscaling Method," *Environmental Monitoring and Assessment* 187, no. 9 (August 22, 2015): 580, https://doi.org/10.1007/s10661-015-4808-8; Robert J. Nicholls, "Coastal Megacities and Climate Change," *GeoJournal* 37, no. 3 (1995): 369–79; Mahir Yazar et al., "From Urban Sustainability Transformations to Green Gentrification: Urban Renewal in Gaziosmanpaşa, Istanbul," *Climatic Change* (August 1, 2019), https://doi.org/10.1007/s10584-019-02509-3; Hüseyin Toros et al., "Long-Term Variations of Temperature and Precipitation in the Megacity of Istanbul for the Development of Adaptation Strategies to Climate Change."

# 2 Tracking cats and voicing dogs

## Locating street animals in *Kedi* and *Taşkafa: stories of the street*

*Yiman Wang*

Watching *Kedi* (Ceyda Torun, 2016) is a consoling experience, as it reminds one of the persistent possibilities of communal caring and sharing—a feeling of hope that distinguishes it from other urban animal documentaries like the New York-set, *The Cat Rescuers* (Rob Fruchtman and Steve Lawrence, 2018). Contrary to *The Cat Rescuers*, where the rhetorical appeal drives and fatigues the audience with the urgent compulsion to spay/neuter stray cats, *Kedi* seems intent on amusing the audience with an overall leisurely assemblage of cutie kitty portraits. *Kedi*'s runaway success also contrasts sharply with *Taşkafa: Stories of the Street* (Andrea Luka Zimmerman, 2013), a film essay that is also set in Istanbul and similarly emphasizes the importance of sharing urban space with and caring for street animals (predominantly dogs), but which enjoyed only limited film festival screenings and no theatrical release anywhere.

If *The Cat Rescuers* forecloses the possibility of street cats' agency by treating them as passive objects to be kept under control, *Kedi* and *Taşkafa* both acknowledge stray animals' agency (to different degrees) by thematizing their entitlement to a free-roaming life on the urban streets, as well as to their unaltered sex. Buffeted between stray animals' independent coexistence with the human residents and the escalating urban gentrification that is erasing urban biodiversity, *Kedi* and *Taşkafa* confront pressing issues regarding the human/non-human relationship in the urban setting, the limits of Foucauldian governmentality and environmentality in the Capitalocene, and the potential of de-anthropocentric zooesis afforded by the documentary form. And yet, different from *Taşkafa*'s activism and free from *The Cat Rescuers*' fatiguing rescue narrative, *Kedi* has found a sweet spot to ponder these issues while also feting worldwide cat lovers and audiences with cuteness overload.

In this chapter, I compare *Taşkafa* and *Kedi*—two Istanbul-set street animal documentaries, exploring their vastly different aesthetic styles, positions of enunciation, and portrayals of street animals, as well as how they address and affect the audience differently. All these aspects shape their divergent approaches to the questions outlined above. In the following pages, I will first map out the theoretical foundations that buttress my analysis of these documentaries. I will then unpack the intricate tensions in each documentary between the soundtrack, mainly composed of human voices and ambient sounds, and the visual track, which traces street animals' spatial navigation, features local caregivers' talking-head interviews, and presents bird's eye view or other establishing shots of the multifaceted Istanbul urban-scape. I pay special attention to the audiovisual and discursive positioning of street animals (predominantly stray cats and dogs) vis-à-vis their human caregivers and the broader history of human commerce, colonization, and capitalization. I argue that both documentaries weave a double text—the humans' and the street animals'—that stages the tensions between the ineluctable human lens (both literal and metaphorical) and a de-anthropocentric impulse. In so doing, they share an appeal for cross-species symbiosis through the voice of the local communities—an appeal that challenges Foucauldian governmentality, veering toward environmentality. And yet, they demonstrate different approaches to issues regarding other-than-human agency and its relationship with human geopolitics. Whereas *Kedi* pushes toward a zooetic experience through a mesmerizing erratic feline rhythm that circumnavigates the capitalist economy, *Taşkafa* enmeshes the audience in a fundamentally human-oriented discourse that subsumes street animals' existence as an epiphenomenon of human history and society.

## Biopolitics, governmentality, environmentality, and zooesis in the Capitalocene

Both *Kedi* and *Taşkafa* get down to the street level to capture stray cats and dogs going about their everyday business. The down-to-street aesthetics convey a strong sense of here-and-now, making each negligible corner and each minute movement unique, poignant, yet also reiterative as part of the animals' navigation patterns. However, both documentaries also reference the broader historical trajectory of human commerce, colonization, capitalization, and neoliberal gentrification as it has unfolded in Istanbul, the centuries-long hub of Euro-Asian interactions. This longue-durée human history has shaped the ways cats and dogs from around the world have been brought to Istanbul, then alternately integrated into and cleansed from the evolving human communities there. If the Industrial Revolution once inspired optimism regarding progress and modernity, such optimism has been replaced by humanity's overdue yet still insufficient reckoning with the aftermath of the Capitalocene that, according to Jason Moore, began four hundred years prior to the industrial age with "the English and Dutch agricultural revolutions, with Columbus and the conquest of the Americas, with the first signs of an epochal transition in landscape transformation after 1450."[1] Moore's shift from the term Anthropocene to the Capitalocene contextualizes our present-day ecological crisis in the patterns of power, capital, and the treatment of nature developed over the past seven hundred years. It enables us to scrutinize the detrimental effects of capitalism, which carries an inherent power imbalance as crystalized in classism, sexism, racism, and colonialism—a power imbalance that problematizes the abstract undifferentiated notion of the Anthropos or humanity.

One outcome of the power imbalance inherent in the Capitalocene is the formation of what Michel Foucault calls biopolitics or biopower. As Foucault argues, biopolitics or biopower emerged in the late 18th-century alongside the Industrial Revolution. It designates the modern nation-state's deployment of "an explosion of numerous and diverse techniques for achieving the subjugations of bodies and the control of [human] populations."[2] Foucault further argues that biopolitics goes hand in hand with state racism (as exemplified by colonization, Nazism, and Soviet state racism) that encourages a battle "not between races, but by a race that is portrayed as the one true race, the race that holds power and is entitled to define the norm, and against those who deviate from that norm, against those who pose a threat to the biological heritage."[3] Such biopower and state racism, targeted at certain human groups and naturalizing a racial hierarchy, amounts to what he calls "to make live and to let die."[4] Biopolitics thus bespeaks power imbalance characteristic of the Capitalocene. If we extend biopower to the regulation and subjugation of other-than-human animal species, then it brings out another form of power imbalance inherence in the Capitalocene, namely, anthropocentrism, or the privileging of human-centered epistemology and interests over the experience and wellbeing of other-than-human animals. Whether focused on "man-as-species"[5] or other-than-human species, biopower facilitates what Foucault calls governmentality that regulates and controls birth, death, health, racial purification, and other vital processes of the human and other-than-human populations.

The art of governing, or of "control[ing] the possible field of action of others" engenders and reinforces a hierarchical power relationship between the governor and the governed.[6] With regard to the human population, Foucault maintains that this power relationship is premised upon those who are governed being enmeshed in and disciplined to participate in their governmentalization. When governmentality gets expanded through biopower beyond the human species, however, those who are governed—the other-than-human species—are less likely to participate in this power dynamic as defined by the entitled human governor. Consequently, the regulation of the other-than-human species often entails "cleansing" in order to ensure capitalist profiteerism in the name of progress and modernity.

When the interests of other-than-human species are indeed taken into consideration, governmentality becomes environmentality. As Timothy W. Luke argues, environmentality "would govern by restructuring today's ecologically unsound society through elaborate managerial designs to realize tomorrow's environmentally sustainable economy."[7] It is premised upon an understanding of the environment as "a historical artifact that is openly constructed, not an occluded reality that is difficult to comprehend."[8] In other words, the environment is constructed by discourses of environmentality as "a nexus for knowledge formation and as a cluster of power tactics,"[9] and it is mobilized to generate "power/knowledge [that] operates as ensembles of geo-power and eco-knowledge."[10] Environmentality thus merges biopower of the human population with eco-power of the environment to set forth "political practices and ideological ideals aimed at environing Nature by disciplining its spaces."[11] While emphasizing the complex interplay of power in the human-environment interactions, environmentality aims to better manage resources for human interests. Within these parameters, other-than-human species and organisms are managed, regulated, and conserved as necessary—but still more or less oriented toward human-defined environmental projects. This emphasis means that other-than-human species and organisms still tend not to be understood as actual entities with their own capabilities and agencies. In striving beyond governmentality and environmentality, *Kedi* and *Taşkafa*, to different degrees, inspire consideration of street animals as agential entities, leading us to engage with Una Chaudhuri's notion of zooesis.

Una Chaudhuri deploys the concept of zooesis as an analytical framework to call for the representation of other-than-human animals as actual entities, with the goal of reversing habitual anthropocentrism and the correlated metaphorization of these animals.[12] She studies artistic works to "identify new means of seeing, showing, and knowing the animals."[13] As seen by Derrida as "this absolute alterity of the neighbor" in his now-famous account of his naked encounter with his cat's gaze,[14] other-than-human animals fundamentally challenge human epistemology. That is, any attempts to know animals qua animals must necessarily begin with the acknowledgment that our knowledge is inadequate, and in many cases, unverifiable. Chaudhuri describes this as the dilemma of a pro-animal zooesis: "How to perform the animal out of facelessness … without burdening it with an oppressive and necessarily anthropomorphic faciality.

Or: How to face the animal Other without either defacing it (as when it starts singing 'I wanna walk like you, talk like you') or entirely effacing it."[15] One approach Chaudhuri proposes, via reading J.M. Coetzee's *The Lives of Animals* (1999), is "embodiment as the principle of a potentially meaningful human-animal discourse."[16] Embodiment enables a "distinction between the seen animal and the somatically shared one" by emphasizing the body, the presence, and the human-animal shared experience as the key to seeking "a reawakened animalculture."[17]

To the extent that embodiment strives for somatic sharedness, thus releasing our epistemological and phenomenological focus from ocularcentrism and the fixation on the face as *the* site of identification, recognition, and connection, it portends more intimate proximity to other-than-human animals' multi-sensory presence and experience. So, how might *Kedi* and *Taşkafa* (or other vision-centric media representations of other-than-human species) facilitate or hinder such human-animal shared and embodied experience? This question is crucial to our understanding of how the audiovisual documentary form could push beyond a predominantly anthropocentric framework.

Finally, *Kedi* and *Taşkafa* are productive examples for considering the documentary form's potential for probing what Donna Haraway calls the Chthulucene and what Anna Tsing sees as the possibility of hope "in capitalist ruins," following the collapsing anthropocentric "progress" discourse.[18] Both Haraway and Tsing seek to unshackle the future from the capitalist grip, and both argue for multispecies entanglements that necessarily build upon zooesis. For Haraway, the "earth-bound" Chtulucene counters the Capitalocene by interweaving "myriad temporalities and spatialities and myriad intra-active entities-in-assemblages—including the more-than-human, other-than-human, inhuman, and human-as-humus."[19] One way to facilitate such "entities-in-assemblages" is to adopt what Tsing calls "new tools of noticing" that enable the "possibility of looking differently" and of self-transformation through encountering and responding to the other-than-human forces.[20]

Bringing Chaudhuri's zooesis-driven performance studies and Haraway and Tsing's multispecies thinking to bear on "street animals" documentary studies, I now turn to *Taşkafa* and *Kedi* to analyze their respective audiovisual aesthetics and positions of enunciation in order to unpack how they reckon with the Capitalocene, and to what extent they facilitate de-anthropocentric zooesis and interspecies entangled experiences.

## Voicing dogs as the "activating metaphor" in *Taşkafa*

*Taşkafa: Stories of the Street*, directed by the German-born documentary maker-critic Andrea Luka Zimmerman, represents an eco-critique of the

Capitalocene. Focusing on street dogs—a marginalized species in Istanbul and vicinities—*Taşkafa* is a film essay that interweaves documentary footage, archival materials depicting street dogs' experience in Turkish history, and abstract reverie posited as a monologuing dog's vision. These visual components correspond with three strands of verbal discourses: the residents-caregivers' narratives of their interactions with the dogs, the discursive explication of both archival materials and the historical sites of dog cleansing, and finally, the novelist-critic John Berger's voice reading his novel, *King: A Street Story*. Zimmerman's interweaving of these discourses yields what Bill Nichols calls the "documentary voice," or "the embodied speech of a historical person—the filmmaker."[21] As I argue below, these three discursive strands occupy variant positions in between two poles—the other-than-human orientation (i.e., intimacy and empathy with the dogs as what Chaudhuri would call "actual entities" and "somatically shared" animals) on the one hand, and on the other hand, the human orientation (i.e., discoursing over "dogs" as a metaphor of broader socio-political issues). The "documentary voice" encompasses and weighs these different positions, ultimately leaning toward the human orientation in treating the street dogs as a point of entry for reflecting upon the broader issues of the power hierarchy in human society and the environment.

The local residents' narratives concur on the significance of cohabiting with and caring for street dogs (as well as cats and seagulls) as a gesture of kindness. Some attribute such kindness to their religious beliefs, while others see caregiving as core to a good communal spirit that is disappearing due to escalating gentrification. Ironically, the residents did not know each other beforehand but were assembled in this documentary through their relationship to the street dogs.[22] In other words, the sense of human community was produced *within* the documentary through the mediation of the street dogs as recipients of the residents' care. One local interviewee demystifies the concept of unconditional care and community by pointing out that while many caregivers name the dogs and seem to bond with them as individuals, some of the street dogs' names suggest a working-class affiliation, and they are given food rejected by pet dogs. The interviewee compares this hierarchy to the caste system that is symptomatic of inequality in human society. The visual footage illustrates this point by juxtaposing well-groomed pet dogs with handicapped, aging, and disheveled street dogs, both passively subjected to human management. Overall, the visual footage refrains from simulating the subjective canine experience, even when the dogs are presented as subjects of empathy. The audience is not encouraged to identify with or "somatically share" the dogs' experience, but rather to observe and recognize them as a marginalized species in need. Furthermore, the dogs are positioned as a vehicle for articulating and reflecting upon socio-political issues beyond their interests and experience.

In other words, Zimmerman's "documentary voice" builds upon her interviewees' voices but juxtaposes them so as to tease out the street dogs' function as a metaphor. As she explains, each of her creative works (including *Taşkafa*) creates "an activating metaphor; an image or con-centration of form that is both actually itself undeniably in the world and also an energising [sic] metaphor of larger concerns."[23] As an "activating metaphor," the street dogs become abstracted into one symbolic meaning—an erased yet "stone-head" (the original meaning of the Turkish word "taşkafa") force that persists against all odds, a force that demands to be reckoned with. By metaphorizing the street dogs and their relationship to the human society, *Taşkafa* ruminates on "memory and the most necessary forms of belonging, both to a place and to history."[24] Thus, for Zimmerman, "Taşkafa is not finally about dogs as such. It is about the way people seek to belong, still and ever more so now, to a larger context than themselves, one which respects other creatures and wishes them to play a significant role in their lives. The key issue is not whether we live securely, especially in its 'official' sense, but rather that we do not lose touch with the shared reality that surrounds us."[25]

This de-anthropocentric yet still human orientation, via street dogs as a figure of speech, drives the documentary's deployment of archive materials that inscribe street dogs' experience (including "cleansing," i.e., killing) throughout Turkish history. One English-speaking inter-viewee historicizes that dog cleansing started in the 19th century as a result of modernization and Westernization. Such cleansing evokes the Foucauldian make-live-let-die governmentality. In a scene that addresses the dog cleansing, we are taken to an island now stigmatized as the "wicked island" where, as the memorial tablet erected by the Animal Party tells us, tens of thousands of dogs were exiled in 1910 by the Union and Progress Party and literally "let die." In this scene, dogs are completely missing, testifying to the decimating consequences of their cleansing. The shots reveal wild landscape and a lone black cat, then cut to Yassiada Island—the site where political prisoners were held and executed in 1960 and 1961, as an inserted caption tells us. This editing decision—sliding from an island where dogs were exiled and "let die" to another island where human political prisoners were executed half a century later—makes abundantly clear the street dogs' metaphorical significance. In these visual and verbal discourses, street dogs symbolize all disenfranchised lives that are rendered disposable by the regime of governmentality. Guided by the notion that the street dogs serve as an "activating metaphor" that refracts broader issues of socio-politics and urban ecology as understood from the perspective of "people [who] seek to belong," *Taşkafa* presents dogs, whether a lone individual or a pack, as the object of the human gaze and an entry point for political or philosophical ruminations.

The street dogs' disappearance into a metaphor is further borne out in the penultimate scene featuring a 2012 mass protest against forcing street animals into shelters—another round of the campaign to cleanse and gentrify the city. We see protesters holding graphic images of suffering animals (presumably mistreated in the shelter). Yet, the only actual non-human animal in this sequence is a large pet dog riding on its owner's shoulder, attracting media attention. Just as the hyper-visible pet dog replaces the streets animals (who are reduced to iconic images of passive suffering), the human-oriented discourse that advocates for non-categorizable street animals (who are neither domestic nor wild) supersedes the actual animal entities. Further indicative of this ironic displacement in a protest ostensibly representing street animals' interests is an off-screen English voice calling on people to give a chance to those who are "different," be it a dog or a cat or a gay person or a transvestite. While the linkage of a dog, a cat, and a gender non-conforming person hints at their intertwined experience of disenfranchisement under governmentality, the lack of explication of this linkage risks cavalier equivalence, thereby eliding the differential marginalization that requires specific historicization and politics of redress. Consequently, the disenfranchised all occupy the analogous position of "strangers in their own time and place," which in turn refracts Zimmerman's broader concerns regarding "the contested relationship between power and the public, and the ongoing struggle and resistance against the single way of seeing and being."[26]

The audience is invited to support people's resistance to animal cleansing and share their criticism of the homogenizing projects imposed from above. To the extent that street animals' well-being is taken into account, such activist and resistant discourses challenge governmentality, conducing instead to environmentality. To recall Luke's argument, enviromentality mobilizes eco-knowledge and geopower along with grassroots voices to create a more environmentally sustainable economy that, by implication, would also foster biodiversity. The focus of environmentality is "environing Nature by disciplining its spaces."[27] The resulting sustainable economy would, therefore, be defined, structured by, and ultimately geared toward human-oriented projects. Thus, the more the street dogs in *Taşkafa* are mobilized as symbolic of all those victimized by the repressive governmentality, as resources to be better managed, or as a taciturn yet vital challenge to the Capitalocene, the more they recede as actual and specific entities who have agentially and perseveringly experienced and negotiated the shifting environment throughout history to the present day.

This human-oriented enunciation is ostensibly counterbalanced by another strand of discourse in this documentary; namely, John Berger reading snippets from his novel, *King: Story of the Street*. This discourse complicates the talking-head interviews and Zimmerman's documentary footage by taking the form of a dog's soliloquy, i.e., a human voice posing as a dog's audible musings. In bookending this essay film and regularly resurfacing through its course, Berger's voiceover crystalizes the central message that coalesces with the "documentary voice." Instead of positioning the dog as the pivotal meaning-maker, the soliloquy re-presents the feat of a human writer ventriloquizing a dog in a philosophical vein. This ventriloquism combines with the aforementioned activist political discourse to lend the "documentary voice" a fundamental human perspective.[28]

Berger's ventriloquized dog takes the form of an orange stray that opens and closes *Taşkafa* in footage showing it lying belly up in the middle of a sun-drenched street, sound asleep with all four legs stretched into mid-air (Figure 2.1). The opening sequence is accompanied by Berger's voiceover channeling the dog, musing over two ways of seeing the sky: "raising my head into a howling position or laying on the back and directly looking into the sky." The introduction of the lone street dog segues to a series of shots of dogs waking up and prowling the early morning streets accompanied by amplified ambient sounds. The objective, observational visual aesthetic, then morphs into a slow-motion

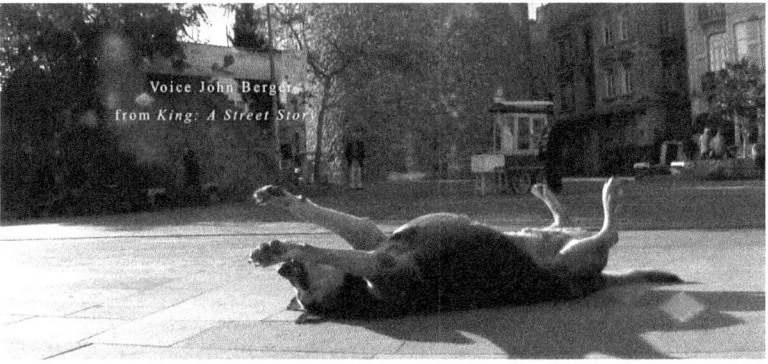

*Figure 2.1* Opening shot of a sleeping stray dog voiced and anthropomorphized by John Berger.

tracking shot scraping across the gray street stone pavers, quasi-mimicking the dog's perspective, accompanied by Berger's solitary voiceover intoning the "mad" dog's reverie of "lead[ing] you to where we live." The last scene of the film reiterates the lone dog lying on the sunny street, this time with Berger's off-screen voice narrating a trapped bird's repeated efforts to break free. At the end of the allegory, when the bird finally escapes with "a chirp of joy," the dog wakes up and walks rightward out of the frame—thus ends the documentary. The closing musings on the dog's freedom to roam supplements the political protest in the penultimate scene that advocates for equal rights for those who are "different" and disenfranchised, including street animals. From the concrete image of a sleeping street dog through its ventriloquized soliloquy to broader philosophical, political, and artistic interventions into the capitalist power hierarchies, Zimmerman develops a "documentary voice" that fully metaphorizes the street dogs to activate a human-oriented critical framework, which then advances a "manifesto for co-existence in film and life."[29]

The three strands of discourses outlined above—the local residents' narratives of caring for street dogs as part of the urban ecosystem; the activist, resistant discourses against homogenizing governmentality; and the philosophizing ventriloquization of a dog's vision—come from different perspectives and occupy variant positions between the two poles of zooesis and anthropomorphism. The "documentary voice" navigates the range of positions, channeling them to advocate freedom of alternative being and belonging. While this voice intertwines the human and other-than-human experiences of disfranchisement, the power of resisting governmentality and the Capitalocene is largely imagined from a human orientation. By deploying street dogs as ultimately a metaphor, *Taşkafa* misses the opportunity of exploring the potential of "embodying" and "encountering" the other-than-human organisms as "somatically shared" entities. If embodiment conduces to "a potentially meaningful human-animal discourse" according to Chaudhuri,[30] encounter is transformative to all those who come into contact, including the human participants, as Anna Tsing argues.[31] Both "embodiment" and "encounter" play a more prominent role in *Kedi*. In the next section, I explore how *Kedi*—what I call a feline version of the city symphony genre—mobilizes embodied encounter to facilitate a zooetic and entangled approach to the urban ecosystem in defiance of the Capitalocene.

## Tracking cats in a feline city symphony

Like *Taşkafa*, *Kedi*'s anthropogenic discourse captured in the soundtrack inevitably lends a human lens to the animal-centered visual track.

In contrast to *Taşkafa*'s abstraction of the street dogs into an "activating metaphor," however, *Kedi*'s human discourse does not subsume the cats' independent embodied persistence to a socio-political agenda. Furthermore, the visual track shows that street cats ultimately exceed the human-oriented discourse. Thanks to the highly visceral and cat-oriented camerawork that approximates the vivacious feline experience of the urban environment, the audience is led into an intimate encounter with a zooetic circumnavigation of the Capitalocene and governmentality. Thus, the resident-caregivers' lament of the dissipating cross-species caring community is counterbalanced by the cats' persistent agile roaming through all spatial and historical circumstances—starting from their coming to stay in Istanbul as a result of human commerce at this geographical site of intersections, leading toward their continuous survival despite urban gentrification and the resulting deterioration of the biodiverse urban ecosystem. If *Taşkafa* advances an overt political activist discourse by diving deep into the street dogs' history and spotlighting a present-day mass protest against stray animals' forced sheltering, *Kedi* suggests a requiem for the disappearing multispecies community while managing to impart a warm and therapeutic affect to the audience by rendering palpable the street cats' daredevil perseverance and the defiantly persistent (albeit dwindling) practice of cross-species, intertwined cohabiting, caring, and mutual constitution.

Like the local residents in *Taşkafa,* their counterparts in *Kedi* also intimately narrate the street cats' distinctive quirks and their own bonding with the cats, which are perfectly visualized by footage of cats scratching the window to ask for food, sitting sideways raising one paw as if to knock the door, etc. The caregivers' naming of these cats based on their quirks further anthropomorphizes them as characters. One female artist implicitly assumes cats' humanness in admiring their natural femininity, which she says is only rarely seen in human females now.

Importantly, such anthropomorphism is not equivalent to self-serving anthropocentrism. As Jennifer Ladino argues in her study of wildlife documentaries, *March of the Penguins* (Luc Jacquet, 2005) and *Grizzly Man* (Werner Herzog, 2005), although marred by the anthropocentric fallacy, nevertheless potentially enabled "love" as "a broader emotional-political category than desire, and as an affect that is defined by respect and ethics, rather than confined to fraught kinship relations between human beings."[32] "Love" as an "emotional-political" affect defined by "respect and ethics" aptly characterizes the ways in which humans bond with street animals in both *Taşkafa* and *Kedi,* especially when some caregivers in *Kedi* talk about encountering and caring for cats as a transformative experience for themselves. The cats' integration into the local plebian life is indicated by the fact that many residents talk about their interactions with the cats while carrying on their everyday business. Such ease of caring cohabitation suggests the caregivers' ethical respect for the cats' independence and freedom from a human master.

Unlike John Berger's voiceover in *Taşkafa*, which assumes a dog's voice only to dematerialize it into a philosophical soliloquy, the human discourse in *Kedi*'s soundtrack fully acknowledges the cats' material embodied navigation of the urban environment throughout Istanbul's history. It leisurely appreciates the street cats as an integral part of the local multispecies environment, worries about their impending dis- location, which will go hand in hand with the community's dissipation as a result of the encroaching capitalist gentrification, *and* holds out hope for a future based on simple joys of living and persisting. As such, it both subtly resists the "make-live-let-die" governmentality and renders an- thropocentric environmentality inadequate.

However, it is in the visual track that I *locate Kedi*'s zooetic potential—the embodied human-animal encounter and entanglement that hold the pro- mise of ultimately breaking away from the anthropocentric knowledge production so as to enable the "earth-bound" Chtulucene that, according to Haraway, interweaves "myriad temporalities and spatialities and myriad intra-active entities-in-assemblages."[33] By analyzing *Kedi*'s visual track to tease out its zooetic potential, I also ask how documentary form might develop a visceral idiom of presentation that is observational, non-human- oriented, and conducive to other-than-human bodily experience all at once.

Orchestrated by Charlie Wuppermann, *Kedi*'s visual style viscerally ap- proximates the cats' embodied navigation of the urban street environment. At the 2017 Environmental Film Festival in Washington D.C., Wuppermann described his rewarding experience of lying on the streets of Istanbul to be on the eye-level with the cats in order to film them from their perspective.[34] In the film, we see frequent street-hugging tracking shots following cats at their height (Figure 2.2). Furthermore, to facilitate the audience's vicarious em- bodiment of the roaming cats, the camerawork highlights the cats' three- dimensional parkour-esque slinking, climbing, sprinting, perching, pausing, observing, napping, and interacting with humans and other cats, then re- enacting the kinetic gymnastics all over again.

Animated by a passion for the kinetic urban streetscape, *Kedi* can be seen as a feline version of the city symphony genre popular in the 1920s—a zooetic version that deconstructs the original genre's cele- bration of industrial modernization and urbanization.[35] The 1920s city symphony genre mobilized montages of predominantly exterior shots of variegated human and machine kinesis to dramatize the escalating synced rhythm of urban modernity and industrialization. *Kedi*'s feline version of the city symphony goes against the syncing and homogenizing kinesis,

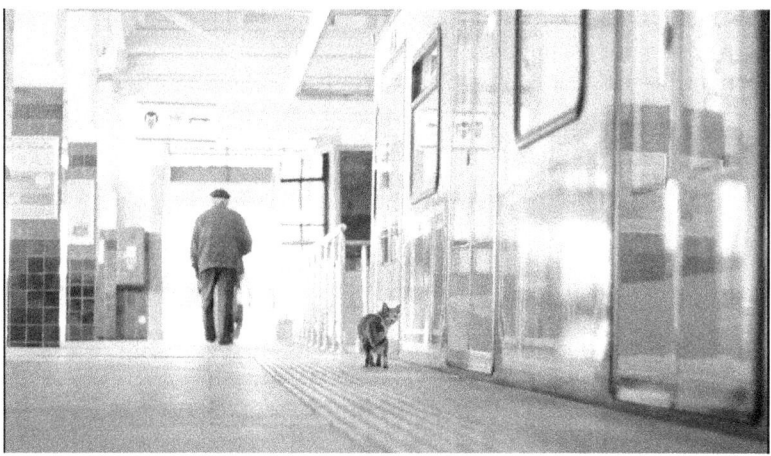

*Figure 2.2* A ground-level, long shot of a street cat looking back as if addressing the camera and the audience while navigating its urban environs.

thus suspending the euphoria of speed and efficiency derived from streamlined and unified human and machine movements. The challenge to the industrial-age ideal is facilitated by the documentary's eclectic assemblage of long shots, close-ups, and mobile tracking shots that thread through all three spatial dimensions at different tempos, collapsing the exterior and the interior spaces and interweaving the human and the non-human actors. Such camerawork highlights the erratic feline kinesis, ranging from sculpturesque stillness to felicitous slinking through the interior and exterior spaces, demonstrating complete indifference to the capitalist notions of streamlining, homogenization, and efficiency.

Many close-up shots, combined with slow-motion cinematography, frame a selected cat in sharp focus, sculpturesque, with crystal clear strands of fur, whiskers, and a glint in the eye. At the same time, the background and surrounding environment (including the humans) become blurred and melt away. Close-up shots, as Derek Bousé criticizes in his study of wildlife film, could risk "ascrib[ing] to animals almost whatever feelings and emotions the filmmaker wishes to assign them according to the requirements of the storyline at that moment."[36] In other words, facial close-ups may induce the audience to anthropomorphize the animal subjects so as to facilitate an anthropocentric narrative. Departing from Bousé's critique, I argue instead that the close-up shots in *Kedi* blow up the cats' facial details without making them transparent or anthropomorphized. The audience is induced to be mesmerized by the feline-shaped microcosmos that remains nevertheless opaque, simultaneously arrested and animated in the very stillness of the framing. The combination of clarity and opacity congealed in the close-up shots defies the anthropocentric meaning-making system, pushing the audience to ponder an other-than-human bodily experience and sentience.

Furthermore, instead of hypnotizing the audience with an escalating speed that sweeps along humans' and machines' movements alike, this feline city symphony unfurls the porous and variegated three-dimensional streetscape through multiple cats' erratic patterns of movements. These movements sometimes intersect, but most of the time, they are independent of each other. Assembled through editing, they remain discrete vignettes that do not aim at a conventional integrated narrative or teleology. The film's camerawork and editing reveal how the cats sidetrack, meander through, or otherwise circumvent the force of homogenization and teleology that drives the 1920s city symphony genre.

In summary, the visual track of *Kedi* effectively captures the street cats' irreducible persistence alongside anthropogenic historical and geopolitical shifts. Even when acknowledging the cats' subjection to the Capitalocene (and the correlated urban gentrification and governmentality), *Kedi* also probes a zooetic approach to the future. The ending of the film sums up this anticipatory gesture. As if defying the shadow of the Capitalocene, a proud whimsical orange cat perseveringly prowls in the receding beauty of dusk, overseeing his territory with dignified grandeur—before a cut to an aerial tracking shot that slowly glides away from Istanbul, thus closing the feline city symphony. If the last aerial shot suggests a requiem for the impending loss of a cross-species symbiotic urban ecosystem, this disconcerting no-future, feared by the local human residents, does not erase (even though it overshadows) the persistent feline roaming and ability to make a home out of any available resources—a spirit of tenacious joy impeccably conveyed through the kinetic cat-centered visual track throughout the film. By exploring the documentary form's ability to present an observational yet visceral approximation of an other-than-human bodily experience, *Kedi* illuminates a roaming space that is interwoven with the history and society created by governmentality (even environmentality), and yet also exceeds complete anthropogenic determination. Thus, the documentary promises a feeling of transcendence, cuing the audience to enjoy and envision a future beyond the menacing Capitalocene.

## Zooesis, the Chthulucene, and the documentary form

Both *Kedi* and *Taşkafa* critique the Capitalocene along with the anthropocentrism that has marginalized animals who deviate from human systems of categorization. They both make appeals for a bio-diverse urban ecology. Paul Shepard argues, drawing upon anthropological work, "what is culturally unclear" is also "perceived as unclean."[37] The street animals in Istanbul defy the clear-cut demarcation between a pet (that is completely subjected to privatizing human ownership) and a wild animal (that roams independently of human ownership and systems of exclusive care), which makes them uncategorizable. They are, therefore, "perceived as unclean" for the purpose of governmentality.[38] Their existence and persistence in the midst of the human-dominant environment enable them to literally contaminate the modern anthropocentric notion of hygiene, health, and progress.[39] Thus, by engaging with street animals on the edges and affirming their value to the overall urban ecosystem, *Kedi* and *Taşkafa* counteract the anthropocentrism and governmentality that would seek to position street animals as unclean, abject, and disposable. They both suggest a turn toward environmentality by calling for better management of inter-species relationships and making space for street animal alternatives.

And yet, as my comparative study demonstrates, *Taşkafa* and *Kedi* hold different positions of enunciation, and they, therefore, manifest varying potential for facilitating the zooetic turn and human-animal entanglement. Their critical difference compels us to ask what language and rhetoric the documentary form might innovate to facilitate the "possibility of looking differently" (a la Anna Tsing) so as to enact what Haraway calls the enmeshed human and other-than-human Chthulucene. The documentary form is particularly fruitful for exploring this issue due to its dual emphases. On the one hand, it is understood to be more grounded in the actual, material prefilmic world than a fiction film is. Thus, its figuration of subjects (or street animals in the documentaries under study) promises indexicality to other-than-human materiality and situated experience. Such indexicality, combined with a structure that defies a human-defined homogenizing teleology (such as the ways in which *Kedi* evokes yet deconstructs the industrial-age city symphony genre through a feline twist), potentially enables a de-anthropocentric and zooetic turn. On the other hand, documentary tends to be strongly discursive with an implicit or explicit argument, which is invariably initiated and filtered through the "documentary voice," embodied by "a historical person—the filmmaker," as Bill Nichols argues.

The tension between these two aspects means that other-than-human subjects are inevitably mediated through human systems of signification; yet a documentary style might push against and exceed the anthropocentric systems of signification by exploring different ways of observing and embodying these subjects as actual entities actively interacting with their historically layered and intricately interconnected biodiverse environs. To put it differently, the inherent tension in the documentary form compels a rethinking of distributed, diverse, and interconnected other-than-human as well as human agency positions across any given ecosystem. *Kedi* and *Taşkafa* both engage with this inherent tension in their challenge to the Capitalocene and anthropocentrism. Their critical difference inspires us to keep probing the key role the documentary form plays in enabling a zooetic approach that will, in turn, contribute to envisioning the human-non-human entanglement beyond the single anthropo-focus.

## Notes

1 Jason W. Moore, "The Capitalocene, Part I: On the Nature and Origins of Our Ecological Crisis," *The Journal of Peasant Studies* (March 2017): 3.
2 Michel Foucault, *The Will to Knowledge: The History of Sexuality*, vol. 1 (originally published in 1976), trans. Robert Hurley (London: Penguin Books, 1998), 140.
3 Michel Foucault, *"Society Must be Defended": Lectures at the Collège de France, 1975–76*, trans. David Macey (Picador, 2003), 61.
4 Foucault, *"Society Must Be Defended,"* 240.
5 Foucault, *"Society Must Be Defended,"* 242.
6 Michel Foucault, "The Subject and Power," in *Power: Volume 3: Essential Works of Foucault 1954–1984*, ed. James D. Faubion, trans. Robert Hurley (London: Penguin Books, 2002), 326, 341.
7 Timothy W. Luke, "On Environmentality: Geo-Power and Eco-Knowledge in the Discourses of Contemporary Environmentalism," *Cultural Critique* 31 (Autumn, 1995): 75.
8 Luke, "On Environmentality," 67.
9 Luke, "On Environmentality," 66.
10 Luke, "On Environmentality," 58.
11 Luke, "On Environmentality," 80.
12 Una Chaudhuri, *Animal Acts: Performing Species Today* (Ann Arbor, MI: University of Michigan Press, 2014).
13 Una Chaudhuri, "(De)Facing the Animals: Zooësis and Performance," *TDR: The Drama Review* 51, no. 1 (Spring 2007): 10.
14 Jacques Derrida, "The Animal That Therefore I Am (More to Follow)," *Critical Inquiry* 28, no. 2 (2002): 380.
15 Chaudhuri, "(De)Facing the Animals," 16.
16 Chaudhuri, "(De)Facing the Animals," 10–11.
17 Chaudhuri, "(De)Facing the Animals," 11.
18 Donna Haraway, "Anthropocene, Capitalocene, Plantationocene, Chthulucene: Making Kin," *Environmental Humanities* 6 (2015): 159–65. Anna Lowenhaupt Tsing, *The Mushroom at the End of the World: On the Possibility of Life in Capitalist Ruins* (Princeton, NJ: Princeton University Press, 2015), 22, 25.
19 Haraway, "Anthropocene, Capitalocene, Plantationocene, Chthulucene," 160.
20 Tsing, *The Mushroom at the End of the World,* 22, 25, 46.

21 Bill Nichols, "Documentary Reenactment and the Fantasmatic Subject," *Critical Inquiry* 35, no. 1 (Autumn 2008): 79.

22 "Andrea Luka Zimmerman in Conversation with Lucy Reynolds: Chelsea College of Arts, London," *Moving Image Review & Art Journal* (November 19, 2014): 233.

23 Andrea Luka Zimmerman, "ERASURES: Being, Seen," in *Erase* (Singapore: LASALLE College of the Arts) 8 (2019): 31. Ecofeminist critics such as Carol Adam critique cultural representations that relegate other-than-humans to "metaphors for describing people's experiences" as a symptom of anthropocentrism that reduces animals to "absent referents." See Carol Adam, *The Sexual Politics of Meat: A Feminist Vegetarian Critical Theory* (Continuum, 1999), 53. Zimmerman, notably, uses the street dogs to metaphorize the erasure of disfranchised populations that include but also go beyond the dogs. By engaging with the paradox of simultaneously foregrounding and backgrounding street animals as a proxy for broader socio-political issues, *Taşkafa* pushes against anthropocentrism while also keeping its anchor in the human orientation.

24 Zimmerman, "ERASURES," 22.

25 Zimmerman, "ERASURES," 24.

26 "Andrea Luka Zimmerman in Conversation with Lucy Reynolds: Chelsea College of Arts, London," op. cit. 232, 233.

27 Luke, "On Environmentality," 80.

28 The inevitable human ventriloquizing of the dog is already manifest in Berger's fiction *King: A Street Story*. As Brigitte Frase points out in her review, King the dog, as a witness and bard, possesses a "nonhuman gaze of pity and mourning for people treated like garbage." Yet, "we're constantly reminded that King really is a pet, who goes around sniffing at hermit crabs and mushrooms. It's just too hard to believe in a poetic dog." See Brigitte Frase, "John Berger's *King: A Street Story*," *New York Times Book Review* (June 13, 1999): 1.

29 Andrea Luka Zimmerman, "On Common Ground: The Making of Meaning in Film and Life" (October 3, 2013), https://www.opendemocracy.net/en/on-common-ground-making-of-meaning-in-film-and-life/.

30 Chaudhuri, "(De)Facing the Animals," 10–11.

31 Tsing, *The Mushroom at the End of the World*, 22, 25, 46.

32 Jennifer Ladino, "For the Love of Nature: Documenting Life, Death, and Animality in *Grizzly Man* and *March of the Penguins*," *Interdisciplinary Studies in Literature and Environment* 16, no. 1 (Winter 2009): 61.

33 Haraway, "Anthropocene, Capitalocene, Plantationocene, Chthulucene," 160.

34 https://dceff.org/filmmaker/wuppermann/.

35 This argument builds upon my earlier, shorter essay on the topic, "*Kedi*: A Feline City Symphony," *Docalogue* (May 2018), https://docalogue.com/may-kedi/.

36 Derek Bousé, "False Intimacy: Close-ups and Viewer Involvement in Wildlife Films," *Visual Studies* 18, no. 2 (2003): 128.

37 Paul Shepard, *The Others: How Animals Made Us Human* (Washington DC/ Covelo, CA: Island Press/Shearwater Books, 1996), 60.

38 Deleuze and Guattari denigrate the pet as an "Oedipalized animal" and a sentimentalized possession that is quintessentially symptomatic of capitalism. Gilles Deleuze, Félix Guattari, *A Thousand Plateaus: Capitalism and Schizophrenia*, trans. Brian Massumi (Minneapolis, MN: University of Minnesota Press, 1987), 71. However, scholars such as Erica Fudge take a different approach to pets' position in the domestic realm, arguing that pets are not just a loved addition to a home,

but are deeply constitutive of the humans that we think we are. Erica Fudge, *Pets* (Routledge, 2014).
39 Interestingly, for Deleuze and Guattari, it is precisely the ability to contaminate humans that make the animal in packs and multiplicity instrumental to challenging the capitalist notion of individuality. As they put it, it is through "expansion, propagation, occupation, contagion, peopling" that the human being encounters the animal," and the becoming-animal is born. Deleuze and Guattari, *A Thousand Plateaus*, 239.

# 3 Foreign and familiar

## *Kedi* and the musicality of Istanbul

*Paul N. Reinsch*

Like much 21st century media, the 2016 Turkish documentary *Kedi* ("cat" in Turkish) presents audiences not only with arresting images but also a complex soundtrack consisting of voices, sound effects, and a range of music. Yet, these sounds are not turned into a seamless sonic tapestry. *Kedi*'s soundtrack includes a rich mixture of six pieces of popular music (five Turkish and one from an American artist), original music by Kira Fontana, jazz from Lloyd Miller, and music from French-Turkish performer Levent Yildirim. This music stages a series of productive collisions between the foreign and the familiar, between musics, between sound and image, and between music and film.

The variety and presentation of music in *Kedi* meet director Ceyda Torun's stated goal of sonically describing Istanbul as a site of merging. As she states, "All of [the music] was very consciously chosen to create the feeling that Istanbul has been, and still is, and hopefully will always be, a place where the East and the West meet, in every sense of the word."[1] Torun and her collaborators present Istanbul as a place where East and West meet, where the past, present, and future of the city intermingle, and where the choice of music, and the treatment of that music, demonstrate that differences are not erased in Istanbul's cosmopolitan space. In the Istanbul of *Kedi*, East and West meet, sonically and visually, constantly and productively, but they do not become one.

As Atom Egoyan and Ian Balfour famously remind us, "Every film is a foreign film, foreign to some audience somewhere—and not simply in terms of language."[2] Perhaps in response to this often quoted proclamation, Tilda Swinton recently wrote: "There's no such thing as a foreign film."[3] While resisting the negative connotations of "foreign," Swinton clearly regards film as the ongoing and welcome encounter with the other through image and sound: "We want to watch things we've never heard of in languages we cannot understand." In one sense, *Kedi* is accessible to global audiences in its entertaining treatment of

Istanbul as a city of cats whose behavior is wholly familiar and seemingly free of national affiliation. In another sense, *Kedi* is an openly foreign film—and a proudly *sonically* foreign film—for many audiences.

*Kedi*'s image track follows a basic organization (the city, a named cat, the people around that cat) that repeats, and the film's use of music is also consistent in its organization. Fontana's score and sound effects are joined with drone footage of the city and other wide shots that often include various (unnamed) cats. When the image track provides closer views of the city, operates at ground or sea level, or features particular cats, popular songs and voices join this footage. For most of the film, songs are linked to specific cats (almost in the manner of a theme song or leitmotif) while Fontana's score accompanies unnamed cats and images of the city. This structure stages collisions between new and existing music and between sounds. However, *Kedi* also alters the presentation of existing music (from diegetic to supra-diegetic), and the use of Fontana's score undergoes a major shift at the end. The specific cats, previously individualized with their own song, are grouped together and scored by Fontana in the film's closing section.

*Kedi* also creatively uses music to address diverse audiences at different registers. The film is potentially sonically strange, even foreign, for all audiences. On the one hand, it declines to translate the lyrics of Turkish popular music, thus overtly dividing audiences between two groups: those who can understand the lyrics and those who cannot. However, these songs are also noticeably altered from their preexisting form by the film's narration in their arrangement, mixing, and even content. *Kedi*'s presentation of popular music is potentially a disorienting, and pleasurable, experience for all audiences. Lyrics are rendered as (only) sound rather than language for some audiences and *Kedi*'s alteration of famous (if older) songs defamiliarizes this material for other audiences.

*Kedi* sonically presents a series of meetings between East and West where the audience's sense of each can change; the film also joins image and sound in ways that suggest these audio–visual components are also always changed when they meet. The sonic address of *Kedi* as it combines the foreign, the familiar, and the (newly) strange invites a consideration of collision and creative friction in terms of culture exchange and in the interaction of film and music.

### *Kedi*'s compilation score: personal and shared

Music in documentary has been a constant presence, even in modes that are seemingly resistant to the presentation of music, such as direct cinema.[4] Like fiction filmmaking, documentary cinema has made use of both music composed for the film (original score) and music, often popular music, which circulates prior to the film's creation (compilation or "pop" score). Julie Hubbert notes that compilation scoring was prevalent in early cinema, including in nonfiction works.[5] Though the practice was largely pushed aside by original scoring, it never fully ceased. And though it was not embraced in documentary as rapidly as by fiction cinema in the 1960s, nonfiction film has come to rely heavily on compilation scoring. Holly Rogers argues that the compilation score in nonfiction film, similarly to its effects in fiction film, can "introduce previous histories and cultural resonances."[6] These histories and resonances can be simultaneously personal and shared.

With *Kedi*, Torun aligns herself with directors such as Sofia Coppola and Michael Moore who seemingly double as music supervisors: "I drew most of the references from my personal favourites, which is I guess what you do as a director, so I can proudly say that of course these were a majority of songs that I grew up with, that I have an emotional connection to."[7] Torun was born in Istanbul and her family resided there in the early 1980s before moving to Amman, Jordan when she was eleven.[8] *Kedi* joins the present moment of the city in 2016 with music that is decades old; Torun's Istanbul (still) sounds like the filmmaker's childhood. Her selections do not provide a summary of Turkish pop music, yet international audiences may experience the compilation score as something like a "Rough Guide to Turkish Rock." Turkish audiences, however, are more likely to recognize the temporal and sonic boundaries of Torun's compilation and to feel the collision between the current images and the old sounds.

*Kedi*'s Turkish songs were all released between 1967 and 1985. While Torun's choices go beyond the 1980 military coup, all selections showcase artists whose careers developed as the Turkish government actively pressed the culture, including the music culture, to engage with the West. This is reflected in the work of several of the Turkish artists featured in *Kedi*.

## "Arkadaşim Eşek" and the kedi who is not an eşek

*Kedi* begins with a visual introduction of Istanbul, and after Fontana's first cue, a disembodied voice makes summary statements about cats. This voice speaks in Turkish and (for Western viewers) is rendered in English as subtitles. Not long after this Sari ("yellow" in Turkish), who is known as "the hustler," appears onscreen. A song then fades up in the soundtrack. After a few measures of music, a different disembodied voice begins singing.

For some audiences, the voice of Barış Manço is as recognizable as the image of Galata Tower that appeared just seconds prior. "Arkadaşim Eşek" (1981) by Istanbul-born artist Manço is also perhaps the film's most famous song; it is the only song mentioned by name in the *New York Times* obituary for the singer, where is it called a "children's song."[9] For Daniel Spicer, Manço is a "tangle of contradictions: an early rock 'n' roller who pioneered synthesizers and embraced disco, and a hirsute troubadour who became a family-friendly establishment figure."[10] "Arkadaşim Eşek" comes from Manço's late family-friendly period, but this does not erase the fact that his band Harmoliner released the first singles of a Turkish band covering Western rock. Spicer directly argues for Manço's lifelong interest in "making musical connections between East and West."[11] "Arkadaşim Eşek" is an irresistibly catchy Turkish song using Western pop idioms. For Western audiences, perhaps only the music seems accessible because, unlike the Turkish dialogue, the song lyrics remain unsubtitled.

This does not mean Manço's song cannot provide pleasure for international audiences; we should not discount the appeal of the voice beyond language. Simon Frith pointedly argues for the pleasure of the voice: "Voices, not songs, hold the key to our pop pleasures; musicologists may analyze the art of the Gershwins or Cole Porter, but we hear Bryan Ferry or Peggy Lee."[12] Certainly one need not understand Italian to enjoy Pavarotti or Xhosa, Sotho, and/or Zulu to appreciate Brenda Fassie.[13] Yet, the song's coming so quickly after the translated speech makes it reasonable for non-Turkish audiences to expect that song lyrics will also be translated.[14] Audiences may check the settings to confirm that subtitles (or captions) are engaged.[15] But the lack of subtitles for songs in this film is a feature rather than a bug. In this way, *Kedi* meets Abé Mark Nornes' call for "abusive subtitles" that refuse the common claim of full, and self-effacing, translation.[16] Contra Tilda Swinton, *Kedi*'s treatment of subtitling, especially in the context of documentary, may feel particularly surprising and even exclusionary.

Torun acknowledges this potential response: "A lot of our European and American audiences don't understand the musical choices; they don't have an emotional connection to any of the songs nor do they understand the language of the words."[17] While the first two issues are difficult to address within the film, the third matter is the logical outcome of her decision not to translate this material. Editor Mo Stoebe reveals that Torun "had very specific ideas on how and where to use [Turkish songs] as the lyrics complement the story at points" while also volunteering that the filmmakers "decided not to translate the lyrics."[18] This decision means only Turkish-speaking audiences will know that

"Arkadaşim Eşek" is a song steeped in nostalgia and, at least ostensibly, about a donkey.

The title can be rendered in English as "My Friend the Donkey" (or just "my friend donkey"). Here Torun playfully hails Turkish-speaking audiences by showing a kedi that is clearly not an eşek (Figure 3.1). The song's chorus repeats the titular phrase, and in the verses the singer looks back fondly on his time with the donkey and asks if he is remembered. The lyrics are perhaps a bit maudlin, yet musically the performance is energetic and bouncy. "Arkadaşim Eşek" moves at a brisk pace and the chorus easily lends itself to a sing-along.

When songs meet film, their lyrics and music suggest many connections and possible meanings. As Jeff Smith writes, "the lyrics of popular music proffer a kind of double-edged sword. Indeed they carry a certain potential for distraction, but their referential dimension can also be exploited to 'speak for' characters or comment on a film's action."[19] Smith also acknowledges that audiences are not identical and suggests two (perhaps overly broad) categories. For "uninformed" audiences the song is "background music pure and simple," but the "informed" audience "will recognize the song's title, lyrics, or performer, and will apply this knowledge to the dramatic context depicted onscreen."[20] Elsewhere, Smith explores irony and humor, as songs create friction with the images and story: "At their best, musical allusions not only serve conventional dramatic functions but also provide viewers with moments of postmodern pleasure."[21] For Turkish audiences, *Kedi* seemingly provides numerous moments of such pleasure.

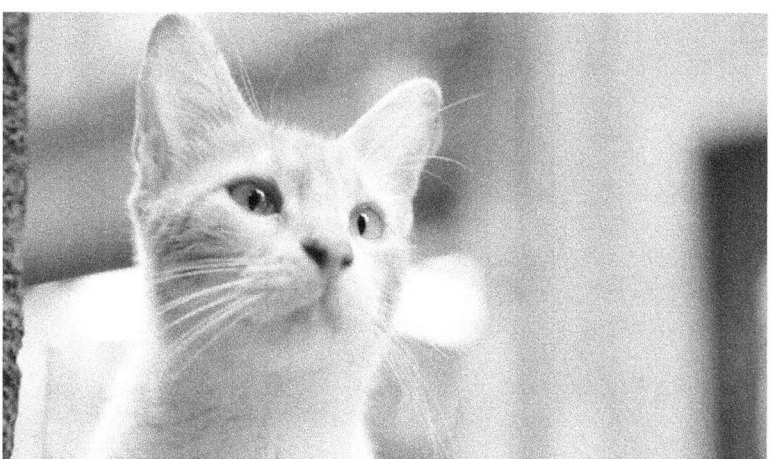

*Figure 3.1* Sari (the hustler) is a kedi rather than an eşek.

Smith's "informed" audience knows the song but also presumably understands the sung language. In both studies, Smith addresses Hollywood fiction film and an English-speaking, if not exclusively American, audience. In the former discussion he offers an extended analysis of the function of songs in *American Graffiti* (1973) to demonstrate the rich and often untapped potential for complex juxtapositions of song and film. It is doubtful, however, that all Turkish releases (theatrical, physical media, streaming media) of *American Graffiti* feature full translations of song lyrics, and the promise of a fully translated and transferable experience.[22] Similarly, Torun's refusal to translate song lyrics is a pointed reminder of the foreign-ness of *Kedi* in relation to non-Turkish viewers.

However, she also denies Turkish audiences wholly familiar ground by changing "Arkadaşim Eşek" itself. Songs in fiction and nonfiction media often intersect with dialogue and sound effects, and volume levels are in a state of constant negotiation. Yet *Kedi*'s sonic address goes beyond this practice; the film actively rearranges famous songs and provides audiences with the pleasure of not only recognition but also defamiliarization.

In *Kedi*, the first and second verses of "Arkadaşim Eşek" play normally. The second verse builds emotionally, with the singer's voice double-tracked, and concludes, "I miss you so much, my friend donkey" ("Seni çok çok özledim arkadaşım eşek"). Normally at this point, the phrase "arkadaşim eşek" is broken into pieces and reassembled to create the chorus. But *Kedi* instead repeats the song's opening instrumental material. Then, as the song's third verse plays, it mimics the effect of diegetic sound as it takes on an echo and the volume drops significantly. The first part of the chorus now—finally—plays briefly at full volume (as supra-diegetic). But the chorus is also changed. In the original version, Manço sings alone and then the chorus is repeated by high-pitched (and presumably sped up) voices that to some north American audiences might sound like the Chipmunks. This is the sing-along the song has openly invited. In *Kedi*, Manço sings the chorus two times and the song fades out without the background singers (or the fourth verse). Removing the high-pitched singing from the chorus removes a core part of the song's uniqueness and memorability.[23] "Arkadaşim Eşek" is less unwieldy without these passages and less obviously a song with direct appeal to children. It is also rendered strange, or perhaps even foreign, to Turkish audiences.

With this song choice, Torun signals her generational identity, and members of her generation are perhaps most likely to notice her alterations to "Arkadaşim Eşek." Manço's 1981 song about nostalgic reflection here doubles as Torun's authorial gesture of nostalgia for her own—and perhaps the nation's—past. She also signals her allegiance with a more widespread nostalgia for Anadolu Psych. This music, with its audio merging of East and West, continues to circulate through literal border crossing that matches its sonic border crossing. Kept alive by Turkish expats in West Germany, and across generations through cover bands and a vibrant reissue and compilation market, Turkish pop is the sound of merging that *Kedi* readily adopts.[24]

## "Uska Dara" and a catwoman singing about a cat

*Kedi* also includes a song from an American artist whose career helped create the market, and ideological space, for "World Music" such as Anadolu Psych. Around twenty minutes into the film, the unmistakable, though initially muffled, voice of Eartha Kitt becomes audible. This is a voice familiar to many audiences, who may recognize it from her sultry version of "Santa Baby," Catwoman from the third season of the 1960s *Batman* TV series, the 1984 dance hit "Where is My Man," or Yzma in the various *Emperor's New Groove*-related texts. Kitt's voice is often described in terms that link her to a cat, and this rhetoric, along with her work as Catwoman, perhaps makes her sonic appearance in *Kedi* over-determined. More importantly, Kitt's voice carries meaning in several languages for audiences around the world. Latria Graham's essay on Kitt includes this mission statement: "I needed to get to the root of the longing that spawned Kitt's signature purr—and the heartache behind the growl that audiences know so well."[25] The purr and growl of Kitt's voice is distinctive as she sings one of her signature songs: "Uska Dara" in Turkish.

"Uska Dara" is an ancient song whose origins are subject of considerable discussion.[26] Torun says it is "probably the oldest song in Turkey."[27] Kitt's version is rendered as "Uska Dara" but the tune is also known as "Üsküdar'a Gider İken" ("while going to Üsküdar") and sometimes as "Kâtibim" ("my clerk" or "my secretary"). As these titles suggest, the song sketches a tale of a traveler (originally male) and a secretary (also originally male), with hints of romance. As the titles also reveal, the song is about going to the area known as Üsküdar, on the Asian side of the Bosphorus River. Though now part of Istanbul, Üsküdar was once distinct (and called Scutari when Florence Nightingale worked there).

The variation offered by Kitt as "Uska Dara" has been recorded numerous times, and at least twice by Kitt (in 1953 and 1960).[28] But the global success and significance of Kitt's version cannot be overstated. Hilal Isler begins to account for both the impact and the enduring strangeness of the text, writing that the song "featured classical, somber Turkish instruments (the kemençe, the ney), but it was also camp. It was a pioneering, hybrid piece we would now categorize as 'world music.'

Without realizing it, in the recording of 'Uska Dara,' Eartha had birthed a genre."[29] If we cannot credit Kitt with consciously creating "world music," we should credit her with appreciating the significance of her gesture. For an American singer, recording a song in another colonial language, such as French, signals a cosmopolitan persona. Recording a song in Turkish, by contrast, had far more complex implications in the middle of the 20th century.

In one autobiography, Kitt explains her visit to Turkey as "the dream of a little cotton picker from the South traveling to the exotic East."[30] She encountered Istanbul (and Turkey) in 1951 not long after the victory of Demokrat Parti (the Democratic Party) and the election of Mahmut Celâl Bayar as president. This Istanbul was more welcoming of Western influence and culture, and Kitt's visit was part of larger, and in some cases government-funded, efforts to bring American culture to the nation. While there, Kitt noticed and admired protests against modernization.[31] She also learned "Uska Dara," which became her first hit in 1953, and which she performed around the world for the rest of her life.

In *Kedi*, as Kitt sings, it is clear that Aslan Parçasi (which might be translated as "part lion"), also known as "the hunter," does not need to travel to Üsküdar because she is already there. For audience members who do not recognize Kandilli, a coastal neighborhood on the northern edge of Üsküdar, the sequence begins with the image of a café and a sign indicating "Kandilli İskelesi" (Kandilli pier). Aslan Parçasi and restaurant workers sit on the edge

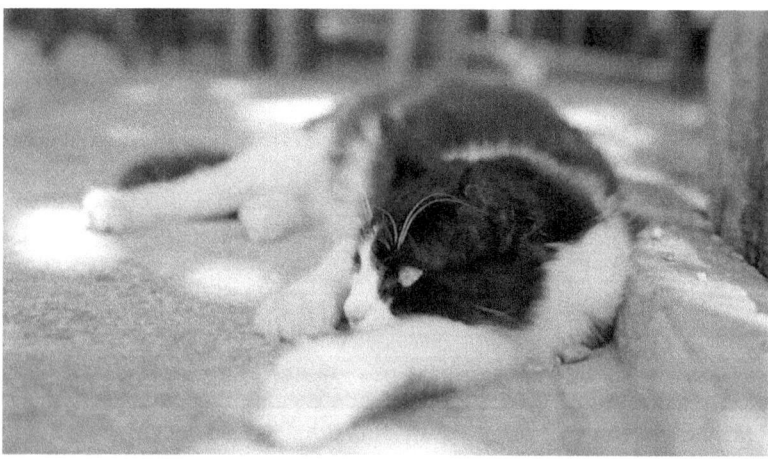

*Figure 3.2* Aslan Parçasi (the hunter) lounges in Üsküdar.

of the water, and she dozes while the men prepare the day's fish (Figure 3.2). Though Aslan Parçasi is sleepy (or at least faking sleepiness), the filmmakers do not include the song's fifth line (also repeated as the sixth) about the clerk awaking ("Kâtip uykudan uyanmış gözleri mahmur").

Indeed, the *Kedi* version of "Uska Dara" is, like "Arkadaşim Eşek," changed significantly. This "Uska Dara" provides the first line (repeated as the second) and then skips to line fifteen (repeated as the sixteenth). Then we hear lines eleven through fourteen two times, the music shifting from quiet and apparently diegetic to full volume and supra-diegetic. The repeated lines discuss finding a handkerchief ("mendil") and sharing "Turkish delight" ("lokum") with the secretary using the handkerchief. These lines seem fitting as Aslan Parçasi eyes the discarded fish scraps, and their repetition—which is not part of the original recording—strongly suggests that Torun wishes audiences to see a link between the song and images. The fish parts are, or would be, a rare and welcome treat (or even a tool of seduction) for the cat. This point of connection also underlines the fact that *Kedi* eliminates all of Kitt's spoken English.

Kitt's "Uska Dara" is a hybrid of (sung) Turkish and (spoken) English. The English sections are very rough and partial translations of the lyrics, which invite non-Turkish speakers into the song's world. Torun omits this material even as the film acknowledges that Kitt united Western and Turkish music more than a decade before the featured Turkish artists. Continuing to respond to Kitt, Torun only slightly exaggerates when she states, "the whole soundtrack … really hinges on this kind of [sic] Turkish pieces of music revisited … with a western flair … or Turkish songs that are westernized."[32] Kitt's version circulated globally, and it helped her achieve global stardom. Its immediate popularity in the United States surprised Kitt when children on a Chicago beach begged her to sing it, and strikingly, asked if she used a "real" or "make believe" language.[33] Turkish audiences, Kitt claims, also told her the song's popularity benefitted the country and "put them on the map."[34]

In *Kedi* and freed from the act of denotation for some audiences, Kitt's voice perhaps symbolizes Western promises of opportunity and cultural exchange. Kitt's voice is the sound of a mixed-race woman born to poverty in the deep South confidently (if not precisely) singing Turkish. Like some of the featured Turkish singers, Kitt's is also known as a voice of dissent, most famously when stating her opposition to the US involvement in the Vietnam War to Lady Bird Johnson in the White House on 18 January 1968.[35] The Secret Service asked the C.I.A. to undertake a report on Kitt the next day, and her career suffered a significant setback.[36] Throughout her life, Kitt refused a monolingual position as she sang across languages and repeatedly declined a monolithic position as a woman or a Black American. In the words of John L. Williams, Kitt was "a black American entertainer who would never allow herself to be reduced to a racial stereotype, who always insisted on her individuality."[37]

For the reasons noted above, Kitt's "Uska Dara" is a logical and perhaps essential text for *Kedi*'s goal, and the weight of Kitt herself—her voice, her body—bridges cultures. Any release, or playlist, with a reasonable claim to offer the "best" of Earth Kitt features "Uska Dara" along with "C'est si bon." As early as 1960, Kitt's *Revisited*, contained new versions of some of her best-known 1950s songs, including those songs and the Spanish "Angelitos Negros." In short, the lyrics of Kitt's "best" music are never fully understood by mono-lingual audiences. If audiences feel excluded, or ignored, by the lack of subtitled song lyrics in *Kedi*, the grain of Kitt's voice nevertheless carries her career-long embrace of multiple languages and musics; Kitt's voice is always an invitation to cross boundaries.

## Kira Fontana's score: minimal music for Istanbul and the cats

Though *Kedi* offers as much new music as pre-existing music, most reviews and critical discussions neglect Kira Fontana's score. Her first feature film score, it bears the minimalist influence of acknowledged mentors, including Steve Reich, John Adams, and David Lang.[38] Perhaps prodded by the context of a documentary film, some audiences may hear the influence of Philip Glass, whose scores for Godfrey Reggio's *Qatsi* (1982–2002) films are justly famous. Using those films (and others) as evidence, Rebecca Doran Eaton persuasively argues that minimalist music in media often functions as a sign for technology and/or rational thought.[39] For much of the film's running time, Fontana's score does not escape these tendencies.

Fontana's music is percussive and repetitive, featuring strings and marimbas, glockenspiels, and vibraphones. The music does not sound "Turkish," and Fontana expresses clear goals that seem directly opposed to previous uses of minimalist music in documentary. As she explains, "I associate bells with spirituality after years of playing Gamelan, a sacred percussion-based music from Indonesia. Ceyda and I wanted an ethereal sound world that captured both the lightness and grace of the cats, and the deeper spiritual aspects of the film. We felt melodic percussion and strings were the perfect fit."[40] Elsewhere Fontana says that she strove to create "an ethereal, magical sound-world to reflect the spiritual role Istanbul's cats play in the daily lives of the city's residents."[41] Overlapping in language, these quotes demonstrate Fontana's goal of musically expressing *Kedi*'s spirituality.

Torun and Fontana pursue this goal most overtly by combining original score with drone footage of Istanbul. Fontana's score plays as the camera floats and surveys in a "God's-eye view." This Istanbul is vibrant but not violent, bustling but not stifling. Istanbul from above is beautiful, and these passages are visual respites from the roving camera and often restless felines on the ground. Fontana's score dominates the soundtrack, but it does not interact significantly with sound effects or speech. Curiously, especially in light of Fontana's stated goals, for much of the film the score interacts far more with birds (and bird sounds) than with the cats. This is logical, in one sense, since the camera is in the birds' space. Fontana's work also plays while the camera is on a boat or viewing the water, but much of this is slow motion footage. Compared to the compilation music, and its occasional diegetic effects, her score seems more directly part of the film's narration. In sum, for much of *Kedi*, the music does little to disrupt the tendencies of minimalist music that Eaton explores. The drone footage surveils the city while also offering largely impersonal and postcard-worthy images of Istanbul. Fontana's music feels perhaps equally impersonal, and its pulsing and ever-steady rhythm sounds as much the result of technology as the slow-motion effects.

Yet Torun gives Fontana's score the last word, allowing it to finally achieve the desired emotional pull. *Kedi*'s concluding montage is scored with a summary cue from Fontana, appropriately named "Moments That Remind Us." Here, the music provides a heartfelt and even ethereal accompaniment to the film's visual recap of the cats, humans, and spaces. Fontana's score, ultimately and emphatically, resists the mechanical connotations of minimalist music embraced within other media. Minimalist music in *Kedi* is defamiliarized and humanized, even as it scores felines as much as humans. The music's pulse is no longer matched with the (unseen) steadily spinning blades of a drone or a potentially dehumanizing modern metropolis. Fontana's score abandons the drone and its links to technology to declare the bonds between the cats and humans of Istanbul.

## Conclusion: *Kedi* as city symphony soundtrack album

*Kedi* is a sonically rich text, and this chapter only suggests some initial approaches to its use of music. The film's treatment of existing—though noticeably altered—music and new music is an integral part of its multifaceted address of global audiences.

The discussion above briefly considers Fontana's score and only two of *Kedi*'s altered songs. While Fontana's score binds the final montage together, the film's final sonic address is Mavi Işiklar's "Findik Dallari" playing for the second time.[42] "Findik Dallari" sounds endearingly like 1967, the year of its release, and like almost any year in the history of rock; it sounds like countless pop songs, and also only like a Turkish pop song. Within *Kedi*, the song is inviting and inclusive and a glance at the band's self-titled LP provides more context. Here the song sits alongside other original compositions and covers of The Beatles, The Beach Boys, and even Rufus Thomas. In the performance and choice of songs, Mavi Işiklar's album combines Turkish culture with Western culture, potentially changing one's sense of Turkish music as much as one's sense of The Beatles. *Kedi* follows the examples of artists like Mavi Işiklar and allows their music to continue its mission in a new form.

*Kedi* therefore suggests at least one more subject for future inquiry: how music circulates after/beyond a film and how its meanings change. Fontana's original score is available for purchase and is accessible online through a variety of services. It is labeled the *Kedi* soundtrack, but this is clearly less than half the (musical) story. There is a nearly complete Spotify playlist (that also fails to incorporate any Fontana cues), but there is no album of the compilation score.[43] Perhaps more importantly, listening to this playlist underlines just how much the music is manipulated by the soundscape of *Kedi*. A soundtrack album that provides the film's versions (the "*Kedi* mixes") of these songs is probably legally impossible, and rights issues have likely presented serious obstacles to a collection of the songs under the *Kedi* banner. Here is a film that therefore cries out for an unofficial (even illegal) soundtrack album.[44] Such an album would feature both songs and Fontana's score. It should be called "*Kedi*: Symphony of Istanbul." It would be a director's personal mixtape, a gateway to Turkish pop, a concerto for cats, and a city symphony without a screen.

## Acknowledgments

Thanks to Laurel Westrup for continued editorial labor, and Bryce Real for research assistance.

## Notes

1 Melis Alemdar, "Hit Film About Istanbul's Cats Finally Comes Home to Turkey," https://www.trtworld.com/magazine/hit-film-about-istanbul-s-cats-finally-comes-home-to-turkey-7498.
2 Atom Egoyan and Ian Balfour, "Introduction," in *Subtitles: On the Foreignness of Film*, eds. Atom Egoyan and Ian Balfour (Cambridge, MA: MIT Press, 2004), 21.
3 Tilda Swinton, "The View from Here," *Sight & Sound* 30, no. 4 (April 2020): 33.

4 Direct cinema, the American variation on cinema verité, prioritizes (or perhaps even fetishizes) diegetic sound. Yet direct cinema practitioners were famously drawn to musicians (Dylan) and musical performances (Monterrey Pop Festival).

5 Julie Hubbert, "The Compilation Soundtrack from the 1960s to the Present," in *The Oxford Handbook of Film Music Studies*, ed. David Neumeyer (New York: Oxford, 2013), 291.

6 Holly Rogers, "Introduction: Music, Sound and the Nonfiction Aesthetic," in *Music and Sound in Documentary Film*, ed. Holly Rogers (New York: Routledge, 2015), 9.

7 Alemdar, "Hit Film."

8 Lyra H., "DOC NYC 2017 Women Directors: Meet Ceyda Torun – Kedi," https://womenandhollywood.com/doc-nyc-2017-women-directors-meet-ceyda-torun-kedi-a53c9ed98bc2/.

9 Stephen Kinzer, "Baris Manco, Turkish Pop Star and Television Personality, 56," *New York Times*, February 7, 1999, https://www.nytimes.com/1999/02/07/nyregion/baris-manco-turkish-pop-star-and-television-personality-56.html.

10 Daniel Spicer, *The Turkish Psychedelic Music Explosion: Anadolu Psych 1965–1980* (London: Repeater, 2017), 113.

11 Spicer, *Turkish Psychedelic Music Explosion,* 127.

12 Simon Frith, *Performing Rites: On the Value of Popular Music* (Cambridge, MA: Harvard UP, 1998), 201.

13 I cannot read or speak Turkish and rely on webpages for access to the song lyrics referenced in this chapter.

14 In some films there is a delay between speech act and translation, as in the first song of *Shoah: Four Sisters* (2018). Later songs are translated immediately with subtitles.

15 Audiences for Indian films, and Bollywood films in particular, are all too familiar with the frustration of scanning the lower portion of the screen for translated lyrics and finding none. For decades Indian films circulated in theatres and home video with speech translated but not song lyrics. Webpages and volunteer contributors for decades worked to include non-speakers.

16 Abé Mark Nornes, *Cinema Babel: Translating Global Cinema*. (Minneapolis: U of Minnesota P, 2007), 184.

17 Alemdar, "Hit Film."

18 Steve Hullfish, "AOTC with editor of the documentary 'KEDI,'" https://www.provideocoalition.com/aotc-kedi/.

19 Jeff Smith, *The Sounds of Commerce: Marketing Popular Film Music* (New York: Columbia UP, 1998), 166.

20 Smith, *The Sounds of Commerce,* 167.

21 Jeff Smith, "Popular Songs and Comic Allusion in Contemporary Cinema," in *Soundtrack Available: Essays on Film and Popular Music*, eds. Pamela Robertson Wojcik and Arthur Knight (Durham, NC: Duke UP, 2001), 428.

22 No subtitles could hope to convey the cultural resonances the songs offer "informed" audiences, which is another reason scholars such as Nornes call for new thinking about translation in cinema.

23 The high-pitched voices in the chorus are perhaps best experienced in the song's music video, as the band delightfully lip-syncs in public. See https://youtu.be/xhltUNCho6U.

24 Spicer, *Turkish Psychedelic Music Explosion,* 237–48.

25 Latria Graham, "Earth Kitt, Coming Home," *Oxford American* 21, no. 107 (Winter 2019): 42. Graham's piece explicitly works to (re)claim Kitt for South Carolina.

26 Bulgarian Adela Peeva's documentary *Whose Is This Song?* (2003) offers a fasci-nating demonstration of the myriad national claims on the song's origin. As she moves through the Balkans, the song's lyrics, instrumentation, tempo, and ideological uses vary widely, but the song's core remains intact. In her visit to Turkey, Peeva highlights Zeki Müren's performance of the song in the 1968 film *Katip* and does not mention Kitt.

27 *Kedi*, DVD commentary. Torun continues, mis-identifying which version of the song the film uses, saying the song "was redone by, or covered by, Eartha Kitt in the 60s. In a kind of a funky, 60s, Eartha Kitt way." Torun is correct, but the version we hear is the 1953 recording.

28 The most obvious difference is the inclusion of very different spoken English passages in the two versions. The 1960 version includes gibberish and English that functions more as commentary than (supposed) translation. For Kitt's own phonetic presentation of some lyrics, see Eartha Kitt, *Confessions of a Sex Kitten* (Fort Lee, NJ: Barricade, 1989), 97.

29 Hilal Isler, "The Surprising Story of Eartha Kitt in Istanbul," *The Paris Review*, https://www.theparisreview.org/blog/2018/10/01/eartha-kitt-in-istanbul/.

30 Eartha Kitt, *Alone with Me: A New Autobiography* (Chicago: Henry Regnery, 1976), 170.

31 Kitt, *Confessions of a Sex Kitten*, 96.

32 *Kedi* DVD commentary.

33 Eartha Kitt, *Thursday's Child* (New York: Duell, Sloan and Pearce, 1956), 227.

34 Kitt, *Confessions of a Sex Kitten*, 240.

35 The coherence of Kitt's statement is disputed. Williams' biography offers a nuanced and well-researched discussion while Kitt writes extensively about the event and its apparent repercussions in two of her three autobiographies. The "Fame" episode of *Drunk History* follows Kitt's version and at the very least reveals that Tessa Thompson should play Kitt in a biopic.

36 Seymour Hersh, "C.I.A. in '68 Gave Secret Service a Report Containing Gossip about Eartha Kitt after White House Incident," *New York Times*, January 3, 1975, https://www.nytimes.com/1975/01/03/archives/cia-in-68-gave-secret-service-a-report-containing-gossip-about.html.

37 John L. Williams, *America's Mistress: The Life and Times of Eartha Kitt* (London: Quercus, 2013), xiii.

38 https://www.theawfc.com/user/kira-fontana/.

39 Rebecca M. Doran Eaton, "Marking Minimalism: Minimal Music as Sign of Machines and Mathematics in Multimedia," *Music and the Moving Image* 7, no. 1 (Spring 2014): 5.

40 Priya Matharu, "Crazy Kedi Ladies and Gentlemen, Just for You, an Interview with Kira Fontana," http://magazine.scoreit.org/crazy-kedi-ladies-gentlemen-just-interview-kira-fontana/.

41 Tom Schnabel, "Kedi: A Sweet Film and Soundtrack for Istanbul's Constant Companions," https://www.kcrw.com/music/articles/kedi-a-sweet-film-and-soundtrack-for-istanbuls-constant-companions.

42 In the Alemdar interview Torun says that she "really didn't know about" the band prior to working on the film's soundtrack, but her selection is wonderfully appropriate. Mavi Işıklar placed second in each of the first two years of the "Golden Microphone" (Altin Mikrofon) contest, a series of events that are in-strumental in the spread of rock music in the country. Beginning in 1965, the competition required musicians to use electric instruments and artists were

encouraged to (re)arrange traditional Turkish music. Finalists were given studio time to record their song, money to press the single, and opportunities to perform in major cities. The contest was created by the country's major newspaper, and the press directly benefitted from the event. See Ergun, Spicer, Stokes.

43 https://open.spotify.com/playlist/6sQ8O1O694Cv14zqVes8Ik.
44 Paul N. Reinsch, "Soundtrack Album Fandom and Unofficial Releases," *Flow*, May 29, 2018. http://www.flowjournal.org/2018/05/unofficial-soundtrack-albums/.

# 4    *Kedi* between the local and the national

*Melis Behlil*

I have made quite a few friends in my neighborhood of Kurtuluş, in Istanbul. There is the tuxedo who waits in front of the shop next door to be let in every morning and extends her head to be fondled when I greet her. There are the two tabbies who are fed chicken from the butcher, cooked daily just for them. There is the slumbering black cat with a sign above his head that reads, "do not disturb the cat, he is sleeping." There is a whole community of them in my building's backyard: cats of all shapes, colors, and ages who occasionally keep us awake during the night with their mating cries. Cats are a part of life in Istanbul, and *Kedi* does an excellent job of demonstrating this, with a clear insight into the lives of these felines, the people who love them, and the city they live in.

In this chapter, I discuss *Kedi*'s "local" aspects. This includes whether the film can be considered a "Turkish" documentary, and the quotation marks should indicate that this is not a classification that I think can be defined easily, if at all. *Kedi* was released in Turkey in June 2017 to great acclaim, selling about 27,500 tickets (a respectable sum for a small independent documentary).[1] Although set entirely in Istanbul and shot in Turkish by a crew of mostly Turkish citizens, the film is considered a US production, with German funding.[2] The production company, Termite Films, and the core creative team of the Turkish-born director-producer Ceyda Torun and the German-born cinematographer and producing partner Charlie Wuppermann are based in the US; they were unable to secure a Turkish production partner due to budget and time constraints. This also meant that they were prevented from applying for any funds in Turkey.

Still, while the film may be technically a US production, the way *Kedi* builds a rapport with its subjects, uses the city's locations, and employs elements of the local culture make it a "Turkish" film when judged from a "text-based approach," to use Andrew Higson's category from his seminal work on the concept of national cinema.[3] But Higson also points out that the very nature of cinema itself is transnational, both in terms of production and reception, reminding us that "specific nation-states are rarely autonomous cultural industries and the film business has long operated on a regional, national and transnational basis."[4] The lines defining national cinemas are further blurred when we consider Tim Bergfelder's observation that, for many national cinemas, their "most valued filmic texts, exemplifying national qualities and traditions"—the way *Kedi* exemplifies life in Istanbul using local markers—"have often been conceived by individuals who are cultural outsiders."[5] Similarly, Jerry White asserts that "not every film in a national cinema […] will be an example of national cinema," just like "some films may not be a part of a national cinema at all."[6]

Where the issue of nationality often matters is in relation to monetary questions. The nationality determines the availability of funding sources for a film, the festivals where it can be screened, and the awards it can receive. Some countries adopt a points system introduced by the French CNC (Centre national du cinéma et de l'image animée), wherein the language(s) of the film, the production company, and various members of the crew count for different points, and films need to reach a threshold number to belong to a specific national cinema. In Turkey, the limited state funding for cinema is only available for majority co-productions (a Turkish production company must provide the largest share of financing). Festivals also have their own regulations, often based on CNC's points system, establishing which films to allow into national competitions that often come with considerable prize money.

*Kedi* had its world premiere in Istanbul at the !F Istanbul Independent Film Festival in February 2016. It was not a part of a national competition, thus avoiding any issues related to its "Turkishness." The film's domestic release came much later, in June 2017. By that time, *Kedi* had already gained international acclaim and had become a surprise hit in the US. *Kedi* opened on ten arthouse screens in Turkey: six in Istanbul, two in the capital Ankara, and one each in the smaller cities of Bursa and Izmir.[7] This is a fairly high number of screens for a documentary, and the film was heavily publicized. For its yearly awards, the Film Critics Association of Turkey (SIYAD) included *Kedi* not in the national category but among the foreign films. Nonetheless, *Kedi* did land in several Turkish critics' "Top Ten Turkish Films of the Year" lists. That the film was in Turkish with Turkish characters, and portrayed parts of Istanbul not commonly found in other foreign portrayals of the city, made many viewers assume it was a local production. Thus, *Kedi* was widely (and mistakenly) quoted as the "highest grossing Turkish film in the US," which undoubtedly helped its local box office. As Thomas Elsaesser points out, success in the US market has often been a way to launch (or relaunch) local productions in Europe.[8] While popular Turkish cinema, which consists mostly of co-medies and melodramas aimed solely at a domestic audience, does have a strong market share of about 50% in the country, for the more urbane and educated audiences that a documentary like *Kedi* targets, international success often connotes quality.

In referring to *Kedi*'s "local" qualities below, I do not mean to inscribe any inherent or essential "Turkish" qualities to the film, but to expose how *Kedi* weaves elements of life in Istanbul into its narration. In this regard, I would call *Kedi* an "Istanbullu"[9] film rather than try to impose a specific national identity upon it. Elsaesser has called attention to how "signifiers of the regional and the local are often successfully marketed" in the global arena.[10] In the case of *Kedi*, these local signifiers are aligned closely with the city, like the aesthetisized cityscapes and the cats themselves, sidestepping any clear identification with a national culture. The easily identifiable local markers may have made the film attractive to global audiences, but there are also more subtle local elements that helped Turkish audiences embrace the film. Furthermore, focusing on this locality and the permeating pre-sence of Istanbul throughout the film highlights the long existing tension between the cosmopolitan city[11] that was the capital of three empires[12] and the limiting imagination of a nation-state.

## A brief history of Turkish documentary production

As Istanbullu as *Kedi* is, the concept of national cinema has its uses as a conceptual tool for contextualizing a film historically. Thus, I will begin by positioning *Kedi* within Turkish film history and particularly the documentary tradition, a history that is interspersed with transnational encounters. Canan Balan points to the anachronism of analyzing "the emergence of cinema in Istanbul within a national context" in the last decades of the Ottoman Empire "when the city was historically so cosmopolitan."[13] Indeed, the first public exhibitions in the empire were organized by a Frenchman, Henri Delavallée, in the cosmopolitan non-Muslim Pera district of Istanbul.[14] Also, the very first films known to be shot in the Ottoman Empire are two panoramas filmed from a rowboat by the Lumiére Brothers' cameraman, Alexander Promio in 1897: *Panorama de la Corne d'Or* and *Panorama des rives du Bosphore*.[15] The latter heavily features the 14th-century Genoese-built Galata Tower, as shot from the water level. Incidentally, the same tower, seen from the op-posite direction and from a bird's eye view, is also at the center of *Kedi*'s opening sequence, as seen in Figure 4.1.

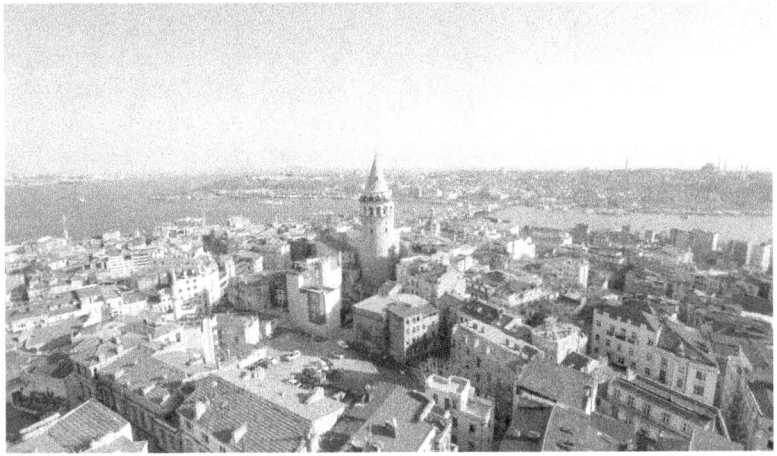

*Figure 4.1* Galata Tower in *Kedi*.

There is much debate on which film should be considered the "first Turkish film."[16] Actualities by the pioneering Manaki Brothers (Yanaki and Milton)—then subjects of the Ottoman Empire—dating as early as 1905, shot within the empire and still available today, appear to be the earliest films shot by locals.[17] In fact, one suggestion for an "official" first film has been the Manakis' *The Visit of Sultan Mehmet V to Bitola and Thessaloniki*, shot on Ottoman soil, by Ottoman subjects, and depicting the Sultan himself.[18] However, the national identification of the Manaki Brothers is another example of how problematic the issue of nationality can be not only for films but also for people: born to a Vlach family in present day Greece, they have been claimed by nearly all Balkan nations as their own.[19]

In the attempts to create a Turkish-Muslim identity to distinguish itself from the multiethnic and multicultural empire, the newly founded Turkish Republic (1923) took on a number of ambitious reforms throughout the twenties and the thirties. Perhaps the most culturally significant of these was the replacement of the Arabic script with the Latin alphabet in 1928. While this may have been a logical choice for a language with vowel harmony like Turkish, the utter and sudden abandonment of the Arabic alphabet meant that future generations would be unable to read any texts from prior to 1928. As Dilek Kaya notes, this allowed for a historiography that "glorified the Turkish re-publican aspects of cinema's past in Turkey," resulting in a "Turkified" history that "has ideologically forgotten the geographical vastness of the

Ottoman Empire and the multiethnic fabric of Ottoman society."[20] Thus, for many decades, the official history dictated that *Demolition of the Russian Monument in San Stefano* (1914), shot by a Muslim-Turkish Ottoman army officer named Fuat Uzkınay, was the beginning of Turkish cinema. But the film has never been seen by anyone, and no reports of its screening are available in the press of the time. This "history" is based largely on one sentence in a booklet from 1946, claiming that the demolition had been filmed by a Turkish officer, as well as several anecdotes that fail to show any concrete evidence.[21] The insistence on this apparent version of history that excludes the Christian Manakis even today demonstrates the need for a Muslim-Turkish origin story for the film history of a nation-state.

In the early days of the republic, filmmaking in Turkey was severely limited. Agah Özgüç's *Dictionary of Turkish Films*, shows only 21 films being made between 1923 and 1938, another 22 throughout WWII, during which Turkey remained neutral until the final stages, and a staggering 77 in the five years afterwards until 1950,[22] when the governing party changed for the first time since the establishment of the republic.[23] These are all fiction films however, and non-fiction films were mostly limited to newsreels during this time. The two noteworthy exceptions were documentaries made on commission by Soviet filmmakers in the 1930s: *Türkiye'nin Kalbi Ankara* (*Ankara, Heart of Turkey*, 1934) by Sergei Yutkevitch and Lev Oscarovich Arnstam, who were part of the Soviet delegation invited to the tenth anniversary celebrations of the republic, and Esfir Schub's *Türk İnkılabında Terakki Hamleleri* (*The Leaps of Progress in Turkish Reforms*, 1937).[24] These films, in the tradition of the Soviet agit-props, were widely shown at the People's Houses,[25] community centers that proliferated across the country aiming to spread the central government's modernist-secularist principles of "republicanism, nationalism, populism, statism, secularism, and reformism."[26] The more well-known of these films takes Ankara as its subject, the central-Anatolian town that replaced Istanbul as the new capital. This substitution was a symbolic move by the new republic: the cosmopolitan world city Istanbul epitomized the multicultural empire, whereas the provincial small-town Ankara stood for the new nation-state.[27]

In the following decades, other foreign (Western) filmmakers made documentaries in Turkey, frequently focusing on Istanbul, often with an irritatingly orientalist gaze. BBC's TV documentary *Johnny Morris Takes a Ticket to Turkey* (Webster, 1960) has Morris traveling across Istanbul with somewhat patronizing observations, which could also be construed as tongue-in-cheek. The visuals range from images of the classical mosques and the Bosphorus to a lively picnic on a nearby island that presents a slice of daily life in the city. The BBC documentary arm often returned to Istanbul—in 1971, 1975, and in the 2000s—mostly with a similar style of a presenter exhibiting and commenting on life in this "beautiful" city with "strange" customs. French filmmaker Maurice Pialat's *Turkish Chronicles* (1963-64) are a series of six short documentaries, five of which portray Istanbul. Beautifully shot with a poetic voice-of-god commentary track in French, the films feature some orientalist imagery of the city with mosques and historic sites, but they also present daily life in an Istanbul that has practically vanished today. Like the BBC documentaries, Pialat does not give any voice to the locals, interpreting this foreign culture from a decidedly Western point of view.

Throughout the fifties and sixties, initiatives by a handful of individuals furthered local documentary production in Turkey, creating a number of documentaries that were shown internationally.[28] The first non-governmental and academic institution in the field was the Istanbul University Film Center (IUFC) founded at the university's Faculty of Letters. Established by European-educated academics Sabahattin Eyüboğlu and Mazhar Şevket İpşiroğlu, the center was modeled after similar institutions at European universities, aiming to create documentaries that would support the teaching activities in the Department of Art History.[29] Active from the mid-1950s until the mid-1970s, the center focused on documentaries about the historical and cultural heritage of Turkey. All the films made in the center until 1960 were written, directed, and produced by the two founders, who had no formal training in filmmaking. The first, and the most famous output of the duo was *Hitit Güneşi* (*The Hittite Sun*, 1956), a documentary short that was screened at the Berlin International Film Festival, where it won the Silver Bear in its division.[30] The center continued its activities under the directorship of Aziz Albek, but the screenings of its films in Turkey were limited to universities, high schools, and cultural centers.

Introduction of sponsorships by private companies in the 1960s gave a new lifeline to documentaries. While the IUFC was shut down for several years after the 1960 coup, Eyüboğlu collaborated with the pharmaceutical company Eczacıbaşı in order to create a series of five short "Culture Films."[31] Although Eyüboğlu wrote the scripts for all five and co-directed one with Şakir Eczacıbaşı (photographer and heir of the company), the other four films were made by Pierre Biro, a professional French filmmaker, who was preferred for his "knowledge of special film techniques."[32] The imagery in Biro's films carries a slight resemblance to the orientalist imaginings of Pialat from the same period, but the voice-over is in Turkish and devoid of any embellishments.

None of the films take place in Istanbul; they either highlight historic sites in Turkey or focus on Anatolian traditions.

Towards the end of the decade, a group of young filmmakers inspired by the events of 1968 across the world founded the short-lived "Young Cinema Movement" (1968–1971), setting the precedent for the political and activist documentaries that would become prevalent in the new millennium.[33] 24 young filmmakers came together to publish a journal titled *Genç Sinema: Devrimci Sinema Dergisi*, (*Young Cinema: The Revolutionary Cinema Journal*), with a manifesto that declared their intention to create a new, revolutionary, and independent cinema for the people. Shooting mostly on 8 mm, these filmmakers documented ongoing protests and acitivites around the country, but their materials were confiscated after the 1971 coup.[34] Although short-lived and local, the group's discourse clearly shows their affinity and familiarity with other revolutionary film movements around the world at the time. Through all of these local endeavors, the focus has never been on Istanbul.

When the state-run Turkish Radio and Television (TRT) started broadcasting in 1968,[35] documentaries became much more accessible for audiences. The British Broadcasting Corporation (BBC) was taken as the model for TRT in terms of programming, policies, and planning; training was also provided by BBC experts.[36] TRT filled its airtime with imported series, commissioned drama series to Turkish directors, but the documentary production was done mostly in-house. Excepting the first few years when it was autonomous (but limited in reach), the broadcasting was strictly controlled by the government, and served as the key propaganda tool for the state. The most prevalent documentaries focused on the cultures and traditions of Anatolia, echoing Eyüboğlu's works, but biographies of revered Turkish figures from literature and the arts were also produced.[37] Any potentially controversial topics were avoided, especially those dealing with recent history. TRT's milquetoast approach to subjects also permeated the films' forms; shallow and didactic films with authoritative voiceovers echoing the state's official discourses have long been disparagingly called "TRT documentaries." TRT's monopoly was challenged by private channels starting in the early 1990s, and it was only in the early 1990s that TRT began developing investigative documentary series on the events from recent Turkish history such as the 1960 and 1971 coups. The new private broadcasting corporations did not invest in documentaries, and television soon stopped being the primary source of funding and exhibition for documentary filmmakers.

With the availability of new technologies in the 2000s, it became possible to have films from a more diverse group of filmmakers.

Previously silenced groups like the Kurdish ethnic minority, women, and LGBTI+ started making and showing films, with the benefit of the brief period of democratization that followed the election of the (still) ruling AKP (Justice and Development Party) in 2002. Topics that had been hitherto taboo, including historic narratives that do not follow the official state line now appeared at film festivals across the country and entered the national discourse. Çayan Demirel's *'38* (2006) highlighted a long-forgotten massacre in the Kurdish-Alevi Dersim region following an uprising in 1937-38 and was promptly banned in various cities. *İki Dil Bir Bavul* (*On the Way to School*, Doğan/Eskiköy, 2008), about the experiences of a Turkish elementary school teacher in a little Kurdish village where many of the children do not speak Turkish, was even brought to the Parliament in support of the right for education in children's native language. While politically less incendiary, *Benim Çocuğum* (*My Child*, Candan, 2013), in which parents of lesbian, gay, bisexual, and trans individuals in Turkey intimately recount their personal experiences, also sparked a lot of discussion in the public sphere and was covered extensively in mainstream media. The increasingly totalitarian disposition of the AKP regime has undercut these developments, however, a subject I will discuss in more detail below.

Also, in the 2000s, Istanbul became the location for a small but noteworthy group of foreign productions, with strong local ties. *Crossing the Bridge: The Sound of Istanbul* (2005) by Fatih Akın, the famed Turkish-German filmmaker whose *Gegen die Wand* (*Head On*, 2004) had won the Golden Bear at the Berlin Film festival just the previous year paved the way for these.[38] The film follows Alexander Hacke, of the influential German industrial band Einstürzende Neubauten, as he goes about Istanbul discovering its various styles of music. Hacke talks to street bands as well as legends of Turkish music, all filtered through Akın's perception of the city. Ben Hopkins' *Hasret* (*Yearning*, 2016) is a self-reflexive documentary about a crew coming to Istanbul to film and discover the city. Hopkins, who has worked in Turkey, is fluent in Turkish, and has a unique insight into the city. In fact, like *Kedi*, his film also comments on the ubiquity of cats, with one character arguing that Istanbul is actually a civilization of cats. In the voice-over, Hopkins claims that the TV channel commissioning the film wanted "time-lapse photography of the crowded streets" and "bustling city life sequences." *Hasret* does begin with these images, presumably what a "Western" eye wants, along with images of the police attacking protesters from the summer of 2013. But it also presents another Istanbul: black and white images of empty streets, nightscapes of a deserted city that is far from "bustling." Leading critic Nil Kural has called *Hasret* "one of the best and most unique films about Istanbul."[39] *Innocence of Memories* (2016) is a collaboration between British filmmaker Grant Gee and Turkish Nobel laureate Orhan Pamuk, an exploration of the city through Pamuk's novel *Museum of Innocence*. The voice-over belongs to a fictional character from the novel, and Pamuk, in addition to being a co-writer, himself appears throughout the film. Another prominent film critic, Mehmet Açar emphasizes that this is a "dark and mysterious" Istanbul, one that the "Westerners are not very familiar with."[40]All of these films diverge from the earlier examples of documentaries produced by outsiders in the 1960s and 70s in that they explicitly give voice to the city's inhabitants; they let us hear the stories of the locals, and try to show a city that goes beyond the Hagia Sophia and the Bosphorus. *Hasret* and *Innocence in Memories*, in particular, overstep the boundaries of classical documentaries, combining fact and fiction in a creative, essayistic manner. *Kedi* seems to share an affiliation with this small group of films. Done with the collaboration of locals or by filmmakers who have organic ties with the city, all of these films let the locals speak, and take the audience to places that go beyond the usual tourist attractions.

## *Kedi* in its national and political context

Having looked at the national (and transnational) context within which one can situate *Kedi*, I would now like to return to the film itself. One place to start is looking at how *Kedi* uses music, a mixture of Kira Fontana's original score and well-known local songs. The film utilizes numerous songs that imprint the documentary with local markers, and their lyrics (often relevant, never subtitled) and connotations resonate particularly with Turkish viewers. Ceyda Torun employed a few criteria for the selection of the songs: she wanted them to be "timeless" like the cats, and also to address the Western influences on Turkish music (and vice versa).[41] In this regard, just like drawing sharp lines to identify a "national" cinema is a problematical and unfeasible deed, so it is with music.

"Bak Yeşil Yeşil," the song accompanying Bengü (the green-eyed tabby with newborns), for example, was chosen because of its singer, Emel Sayın. In addition to singing, she also played in movies, sappy melodramas of popular Turkish cinema that the men who take care of Bengü refer to. In a fortunate coincidence, the lyrics translate loosely as "look at me with your green eyes," making it a perfect match for this sequence on multiple levels. All the other songs reflect the cross-cultural influences Torun refers to. Three of them belong to the Anatolian-rock genre, a fusion of Turkish folk and rock music, emerging in the mid-60s.

Barış Manço's "Arkadaşım Eşek" ("My Friend, the Donkey") appears in the sequence about Sarı, Erkin Koray's "Deli Kadın" ("Crazy Woman") plays fittingly in the background while Psikopat (Psycho) terrorizes the neighborhood, and a flirty folk song reinterpreted in the style of the early Beatles by the band Mavi Işıklar plays as the closing song. The fact that these musicians have been inspired by Western rock is obvious, but what may not be as widely known is that Anatolian-rock has become popular across Europe in the 2000s as "Turkish Psychedelia," demonstrating that cultural exchanges do not need to be, and often are not, simply unidirectional.[42]

While not in the same style, MFÖ's "Peki Peki Anladık" ("Alright, We Get It") introducing Duman (Smokey), the restaurant cat feeding on Manchego cheese, lies also within a Western pop music tradition. In 1985 and 1988, MFÖ represented Turkey at the Eurovision Song Contest, creating a small but solid fan base for itself in Europe. The only "Western" recording in the film plays while Aslan Parçası (Little Lion) hunts rats along the Bosphorus: Eartha Kitt's rendition of an Ottoman Turkish song, "Üsküdar'a Gider İken," as "Uska Dara," which was the African American singer's first big hit in 1953.[43] Kitt had performed in Istanbul previously, and this was an example of "the kind of exotic, foreign-language novelty song" she would become associated with throughout her career.[44] For the Turkish audiences, all these pieces of music create a familiarity that Fontana's score alone would not afford. The soundtrack of *Kedi* reflects a multicultural soundscape that local audiences can clearly identify with Istanbul.

Other elements of the film that are uniquely recognizable to local audiences are the human characters and locations. Several of the individuals are known figures, including a writer, an actress, and most notably, a cartoonist whose work underlines the significance of cats in the Turkish consciousness. Bülent Kaptan, seen here drawing a chubby tabby, is the creator of *Kötü Kedi Şerafettin* (*Bad Cat*), easily the most celebrated cartoon character in Turkey. A subversive character inspired by Robert Crumb's "Fritz the Cat," Şerafettin is a womanizer and a thief who smokes, drinks, and uses drugs. He's the product of an accident involving a feline mother and a masturbating human father. The strip, which started publication in *L-Manyak* humor magazine in 1996, has been known to rely on "exaggerated violence, sex and action."[45] Humor magazines have long been hugely popular in Turkey; comics characters are not marginalized cult figures but rather occupy a strong position within the pop culture. Moreover, Şerafettin happens to live with his friends in Cihangir, where *Kedi*'s Gamsız (Carefree) also resides.

He is not only distinctly Istanbullu, he is an integral part of this neighborhood, where cat food is neatly served along the sidewalks.

Cihangir lies on the edge of Pera, which in addition to the old city and the Bosphorus, is the most internationally recognized region of the city. Galata Tower, from the opening shots, is also in this district. But despite the use of the somewhat-clichéd bird's eye view images of the tower, *Kedi* quickly moves to other parts of the city and provides stories and images from distinct regions of Istanbul. By documenting some of these areas, *Kedi* functions as an archive for the memory of the rapidly transforming city. The market where Deniz lives, in the sequence that frames the discussions on urban renewal, is lucky to still be standing, but large parts of the waterfront area where Bengü resides have been demolished.

The mood of the city has also significantly shifted since the time *Kedi* was made. While some critics have argued that lack of politics in the film is its weak point, *Kedi* does reflect on the psyche of its time. Early in the film, there is graffiti clearly visible on the walls that reads "Erdo-Gone," referring to the then-prime minister, later president Recep Tayyip Erdoğan. *Kedi* was shot mostly in 2014, barely a year after the Gezi protests, when a wave of civil unrest and peaceful protests swept the country.[46] Nonetheless, there did not seem to be a significant change in how the country was run, and this seems to be what one of the characters refers to when she talks about rekindling "our slowly dying joy of life." Things took a turn for the worse in 2015, with terror attacks across Istanbul and renewed fighting in the Southeast following a brief armistice with Kurdish guerillas.[47] Following an unsuccessful coup attempt in July 2016, a State of Emergency was declared, and there was a harsh crackdown on any oppositional voices resulting in hundreds of thousands of people being removed from their jobs, and thousands being jailed.[48] Many were brought to court on arbitrary charges of being "members of a terrorist group," many more for "spreading terrorist propaganda," and thousands who expressed their discontent with the head of state have been charged with "insulting the President."[49]

The documentary filmmaking scene in Turkey has been strongly marked by these authoritarian actions. The (already inadequate) funding provided for documentaries by the Ministry of Culture became extremely politicized, weeding out any potentially critical films and any dissenting names. Its sole alternative, the New Film Fund, was established in 2015 by the Anadolu Kültür Foundation but had to be suspended in 2018 after the founder of Anadolu Kültür, Osman Kavala, was jailed on vague charges of "attempting to overthrow the government."[50]

Television companies had never invested greatly in documentaries anyway, and nearly all media channels have been taken over by pro-government businesses that will not allow any independent voices.[51]

Film festivals, the main outlet for theatrical documentaries, have become sites of contestation between the government and the filmmakers. In 2014, Antalya Film Festival—the oldest in the country—fell into turmoil when three members of the pre-selection committee announced that a documentary about the Gezi protests called *Yeryüzü Aşkın Yüzü Oluncaya Dek* (*Love Will Change the Earth*, Tuvi, 2014), selected for the competition, was to be removed from the program by the festival. The committee resigned, followed by all the members of the competition jury. The reasoning behind the removal was that the film could constitute the crime of "insulting the president" (as there is one scene where chants against the president can be heard in the background), and that the festival "wanted to protect the film." Nearly all films in the documentary competition were withdrawn, effectively and officially cancelling the competition. Antalya Film Festival, run by a municipality with an AKP mayor, canceled the national documentary competition entirely the following year.[52] In 2015, Istanbul Film Festival was asked by the Ministry of Culture to remove *Bakur* (*North*, 2015) from its program, resulting in the cancellation of the competition.[53] *Bakur* documents the camps of PKK, the Kurdish separatist group that is considered a terrorist organization by Turkey, the US, and NATO. Since then, filmmakers Çayan Demirel and Ertuğrul Mavioğlu have been tried and sentenced to four and a half years in prison for spreading terrorist propaganda.[54]

*Kedi* did not have to deal with such restrictions, but it was not entirely isolated from politics either. Around the time of its release in June 2017, a culture and arts magazine published by the municipality of Istanbul (then run by AKP) ran a cover story on Istanbul's cats, also discussing the film. One of the featured images included the "Erdo-Gone" graffiti (Figure 4.2), creating a scandal among the pro-government press. The journal was promptly shut down, its remaining copies withdrawn from the shelves, and its editor, editorial coordinator in charge of content, and editor-in-chief fired. Then-mayor Kadir Topbaş said he was "appalled" and added "necessary precautions have been taken. They shall answer at the court for what they did."[55]

*Kedi* itself was somehow shielded from this dispute. The pro-government press, always quick to attack anyone in contempt of Erdoğan, attacked the magazine but not the film. Perhaps the publication of the image was the manifestation of ongoing conflicts within the

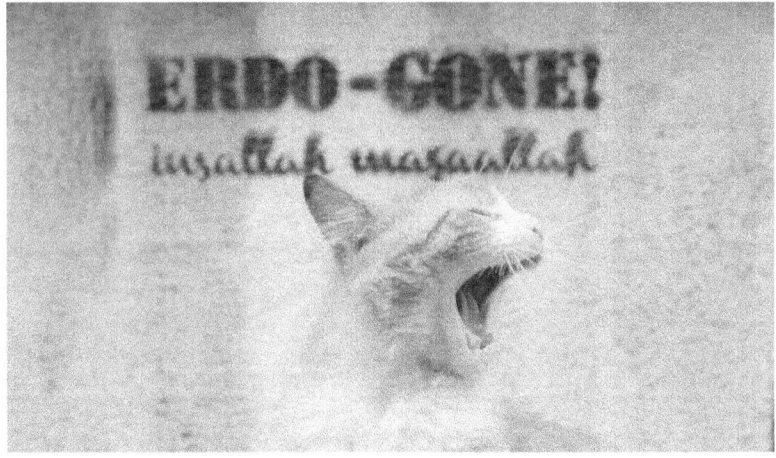

*Figure 4.2* Dangerous graffiti in *Kedi*.

ruling party, and the image from the film was just a tool that happened to give ammunition to one of the conflicting factions. It is also likely that a documentary that came out only on a handful of arthouse screens was not seen as a serious threat. The lack of a familiarity with documentaries on the part of those attacking the magazine may have led them to believe that a documentary just showed "what was out there," and such graffiti was a part of the city at that time. But the inclusion of it in the film, and the usage of it as promotional material is a deliberate choice by the filmmaker that positions the film, the city, and the cats in opposition to the "national" politics based in Ankara.

*Kedi* may be variably seen by different constituencies as a US or a Turkish documentary, but it goes beyond a national discourse; as a transnational documentary, it looks at Istanbul from the outside, with access to international flows of financing and distribution, while possessing the knowledge of an insider. It can be seen as a Turkish film as far as its language and themes go, but by focusing on the city and underlining the multicultural elements within the city's culture, it is more Istanbullu than anything else. By virtue of a country being physically larger than a city, being defined as an Istanbullu film might seem more limiting than as a Turkish or American film. Nonetheless, from its opening lines to various cultural references, *Kedi* positions itself within this ancient capital with a vast history, even if it is not speaking specifically of this history and reaches for something greater than alignment within a national discourse.

# Notes

1 "Kedi – Box Office Türkiye," accessed January 26, 2020, https://boxofficeturkiye.com/film/kedi-2013541.
2 Ceyda Torun, Skype interview with the author, January 24, 2020.
3 Andrew Higson, "The Concept of National Cinema," *Screen* 30, no. 4 (1989): 36–47, 36.
4 Andrew Higson, "The Limiting Imagination of National Cinema," in *Cinema and Nation*, eds. Mette Hjort and Scott MacKenzie (London and New York: Routledge, 2000), 63–74, 67.
5 T. Bergfelder, "National, Transnational or Supranational Cinema? Rethinking European Film Studies," *Media, Culture & Society* 27, no. 3 (2005): 315–31, 320.
6 Jerry White, "National Belonging," *New Review of Film and Television Studies* 2, no. 2 (2004): 211–32, 228.
7 Deniz Aytekin, "Amerika'da Gişe Rekorları Kıran Kedi Filmi Bugün Vizyona Giriyor," Yeşilist, June 9, 2017, https://www.yesilist.com/amerikada-gise-rekorlari-kiran-kedi-filmi-bugun-vizyona-giriyor/.
8 Thomas Elsaesser, *European Cinema: Face to Face with Hollywood* (Amsterdam: Amsterdam University Press, 2005), 493.
9 What the locals of Istanbul are called in Turkish.
10 Elsaesser, *European Cinema: Face to Face with Hollywood*, 19.
11 Edhem Eldem underlines the problems of calling Istanbul "cosmopolitan" even in the Ottoman period. See Edhem Eldem, "Istanbul as a Cosmopolitan City," in *A Companion to Diaspora and Transnationalism*, eds. Ato Quayson and Girish Daswani (West Sussex: Wiley Blackwell, 2013), 212–45. During the republican era, Istanbul's population ballooned as the non-Muslim minorities left the city, resulting in a more homogenous populace. I employ the term to distinguish Istanbul from the capital Ankara and the nation-building ideals that Ankara is associated with.
12 Roman (330–395), Byzantine (395–1453), and Ottoman (1453–1923).
13 Canan Balan, "Wondrous Pictures in Istanbul: From Cosmopolitanism to Nationalism," in *Early Cinema and the "National,"* eds. Richard Abel, Giorgio Bertellini, and Rob King (Herts: John Libbey Publishing, 2008), 170–82, 172.
14 Nezih Erdoğan, "The Spectator in the Making: Modernity and Cinema in Istanbul, 1896–1928," in *Orienting Istanbul: Cultural Capital of Europe?*, eds. Deniz Göktürk, Levent Soysal, and Ipek Tureli (Oxfordshire & New York: Routledge, 2010), 145–59, 131.
15 Ahmet Gürata, "City of Intrigues. Istanbul as an Exotic Attraction," in *World Film Locations: Istanbul*, ed. Özlem Köksal (Bristol: Intellect Books, 2012), 24–41, 24. Both films are available in the Lumière Catalogue, https://catalogue-lumiere.com/.
16 Hakan Aytekin, "Belgesel Sinemamıza 'Milat' Seçmek," in *Belgesel Sinema 2009–2010*, ed. Hakan Aytekin (Istanbul: Belgesel Sinemacılar Birliği, 2011), 60.
17 Saadet Özen, "'Balkanlar'ın İlk Sinemacıları' Mı?: Manaki Biraderler," *Toplumsal Tarih*, no. 219 (2012): 60–67.
18 Burçak Evren, *Sigmund Weinberg: Türkiye'ye Sinemayı Getiren Adam* (Istanbul: Milliyet Yayınları, 1995), 68.
19 Marian Tutui, "Balkan Cinema versus Cinema of the Balkan Nations," http://aqshf.gov.al/uploads/2.___Manakia_Bros_Pioneers_of_Balkan_Cinema_Claimed_by_Six_Nations.pd.

20  Dilek Kaya, "Remembering the First Movie Theaters and Early Cinema Exhibition in Quay, Smyrna, Turkey," in *The Routledge Companion to New Cinema History*, eds. Daniel Biltereyst, Richard Maltby, and Phillippe Meers (London and New York: Routledge, 2019), 244–53, 245.

21  Dilek Kaya Mutlu, "The Russian Monument at Ayastefanos (San Stefano): Between Defeat and Revenge, Remembering and Forgetting," *Middle Eastern Studies* 43, no. 1 (January 2007): 75–86, 80.

22  Agah Özgüç, *Türk Filmleri Sözlüğü*, 3rd ed. (Istanbul: Horizon International, 2012).

23  This number would grow enormously until the mid-1970s, creating the successful Turkish film industry known as "Yeşilçam" (Green Pine).

24  Hakan Aytekin, *Türkiyede Toplumsal Değişme ve Belgesel Sinema* (Istanbul: Belgesel Sinemacılar Birliği, 2016), 80. Schub's footage is from the same year, however, it took three years to complete editing. *Ankara* is available on YouTube.

25  Savaş Arslan, *Cinema in Turkey: A New Critical History* (Oxford: Oxford University Press, 2011), 41.

26  Kemal H Karpat, "The People's Houses in Turkey: Establishment and Growth," *Middle East Journal* 17, no. 1/2 (1963): 55–67, 58.

27  Kyle T Evered, "Symbolizing a Modern Anatolia: Ankara as Capital in Turkey's Early Republican Landscape," *Comparative Studies of South Asia, Africa and the Middle East* 28, no. 2 (2008): 326–41.

28  Can Candan, "Documentary Cinema in Turkey: A Brief Survey of the Past and the Present," in *The City in Turkish Cinema*, eds. Hakkı Başgüney and Özge Özdüzen (Istanbul: Libra Kitap, 2014), 113–34, 116.

29  Aytekin, *Türkiyede Toplumsal Değişme ve Belgesel Sinema*, 96.

30  Aytekin, 127.

31  Can Candan, "Kültür Filmleri," *Altyazı*, June 2010.

32  Aytekin, *Türkiyede Toplumsal Değişme ve Belgesel Sinema*, 133.

33  Candan, "Documentary Cinema in Turkey," 117.

34  Mesut Kara, "Sinematek ve Genç Sinema Hareketi," *Evrensel*, April 6, 2013, https://www.evrensel.net/yazi/53522/sinematek-ve-genc-sinema-hareketi.

35  Although TRT's experimental broadcasts began in 1968, the network did not expand until the early 1970s. By 1974, 55% of the population had access to network television."Tarihçe (History)," accessed May 30, 2020, https://www.trt.net.tr/Kurumsal/Tarihce.aspx.

36  Tülin Seyhan Ceylan, "Policies of Turkish Radio Television Corporation (TRT): The Case of the Directorate of Documentary Programs" (Middle East Technical University, 2006), 93. http://etd.lib.metu.edu.tr/upload/3/12607297/index.pdf.

37  Aytekin, *Türkiyede Toplumsal Değişme ve Belgesel Sinema*, 149.

38  *Crossing the Bridge* was released in many European countries, the US, Brazil, Uruguay, and Japan, surpassing $700,000 globally, https://www.boxofficemojo.com/title/tt0459242/.

39  Nil Kural, "Kayıp İstanbul'un Izindeki Belgesel," *Milliyet*, March 12, 2016, https://www.milliyet.com.tr/yazarlar/nil-kural/kayip-istanbul-un-izindeki-belgesel-2208208.

40  Mehmet Açar, "Roman, Müze ve Film," *Habertürk*, March 27, 2016, https://www.haberturk.com/yazarlar/mehmet-acar/1215784-roman-muze-ve-film.

41  Most of the songs come from the 1970s and the 1980s, helping to re-create the soundscape of the filmmaker's childhood in Istanbul, which she repeatedly cites as her main inspiration.

42 Setenay Gültekin, "Turkish Psychedelia: The Revival of Anatolian Pop" (Kadir Has University, 2019), http://academicrepository.khas.edu.tr/bitstream/handle/20.500.12469/2771/Turkish, psychedelia the revival of Anatolian pop.pdf?sequence=1&isAllowed=y.

43 The song is claimed by all nations in the region. There is a documentary that travels from the Balkans toward Turkey, tracing the origins of the tune: *Whose Is This Song* (Peeva, 2003).

44 Colleen Kim Daniher, "Yella Gal: Eartha Kitt's Racial Modulations," *Women & Performance: A Journal of Feminist Theory* 28, no. 1 (2018): 16–33, 20.

45 Turhan Yalçınkaya, "A Shift in the Tradition of Humour Magazines in Turkey: The Case of L-Manyak and Lombak" (Middle East Technical University, 2006), 78. https://etd.lib.metu.edu.tr/upload/12608118/index.pdf.

46 The spark of the protests was the planned demolition of Gezi Park in the Pera district.

47 "Wave of Terror Attacks in Turkey Continue at a Steady Pace," *The New York Times*, 2016, https://www.nytimes.com/interactive/2016/06/28/world/middleeast/turkey-terror-attacks-bombings.html.

48 "Turkey's Failed Coup Attempt: All You Need to Know," 2017, https://www.aljazeera.com/news/2016/12/turkey-failed-coup-attempt-161217032345594.html.

49 "Turkish Court Cases over 'Insulting' the President up 30% in 2018," *Middle East Eye*, 2019, https://www.middleeasteye.net/news/26000-people-investigated-insulting-erdogan-2018.

50 "Turkey Sends Philanthropist Back to Prison despite European Ruling," *Al-Monitor*, 2020, https://www.al-monitor.com/pulse/originals/2020/01/turkish-court-osman-kavala-prison-defy-un-human-rights-court.html.

51 In the post-TRT era, only news channels and one cable documentary channel (İz TV, from 2006) screened and produced documentaries. Al Jazeera network established an office in Turkey in the early 2010s and commissioned documentaries but shut down operations in 2017. These were not theatrically released creative documentaries.

52 When the municipality changed hands in 2019, the documentary competition was reintroduced.

53 "Film-Makers Withdraw from Istanbul Festival in Censorship Protest," *The Guardian*, 2015, https://www.theguardian.com/world/2015/apr/13/film-makers-withdraw-films-istanbul-film-festival.

54 Their case is at Regional Court of Justice for the appellate hearing as of mid-2020.

55 "İstanbul Municipality Closes Magazine Due to Cat Photo," bianet.org, 2017, http://bianet.org/english/freedom-of-expression/186510-istanbul-municipality-closes-magazine-due-to-cat-photo?bia_source=rss.

# 5 *Kedi*

## Crossover documentary as popular art cinema

*Chris Cagle*

During a question-and-answer session promoting her film *Kedi* (2016), director Ceyda Torun remarked how the documentary was a surprise choice for a first feature project for her and her collaborator Charlie Wuppermann:

> You know it's funny, my background is more narrative stuff and I didn't really even think that my first film would be a documentary, but I'm super glad that it was. Because it's a form of filmmaking that influences everything else that you do. But I think for sure my, and my cinematographer Charlie's backgrounds are in narrative film. Even more sort of like 'classically' narrative film, in terms of the look of the project. We made a great effort for it to look as 'filmic' as possible, because that's what we like.[1]

Torun is hardly the first documentary director with an interest and background in fiction filmmaking, and she is in good company with many documentary filmmakers increasingly seeking an aestheticized approach. Therefore, the statement reveals a tension in *Kedi*'s aesthetic sensibility between a traditional documentary project, based on observational shooting, and an aspiration toward qualities identified with the "filmic": high production values, pictorial cinematography, and rich sound design.

However, even if many directors cross between fiction and documentary filmmaking—and even if the cross-pollination has a very long history—*Kedi* reflects some of the particular challenges and successes of documentaries in the current "post-cinema" moment of the media industries.[2] As video streaming is fundamentally changing the economics of distribution, films like *Kedi* have managed to find decent distribution and a good financial return. Using *Kedi*'s theatrical release year of 2017 and the United States' context as an industrial case study, this essay proposes that *Kedi* occupies a particular niche in the distribution sphere, that of the "crossover documentary," the nonfiction equivalent of "popular art cinema." *Kedi*'s US box-office performance corresponds to its position in between popular cinema and indie or art cinema. Stylistically, too, the documentary is a melding of each. In many respects, the specific stylistic mix of *Kedi* is distinctive, but the film reflects a broader and growing crossover documentary sensibility and speaks to the challenges of documentary distribution in the late 2010s.

## 2017: a snapshot of documentary distribution

In the United States and globally, film distribution has faced simultaneous consolidation and disruption in the past several decades. The US film industry has long been centered on an oligopoly of production and distribution. Since the late 1990s, the industry has consolidated with major media corporations in order to dominate market share and gain synergy, so that most of the major studios (Disney, Warner Bros., 20th Century-Fox, Universal, Sony, and Paramount) belong to larger media conglomerations, with the additional acquisition of 20th Century-Fox by Disney in 2018. The focus on synergy has led the major studios to prioritize bigger budget and lower risk productions, particularly "tentpole" and franchise films; these dominate the release calendar from the majors.[3] The majors' preference has come at the cost of the middle-budget picture; meanwhile, the mini-boom in the independent cinema of the 1990s retrenched. Mini-major studios, true independent distributors, and majors' specialty divisions did not disappear, but many closed down, leading many industry commentators to identify a crisis in independent cinema.[4] In 2017, the box office hierarchy was stark: the (then) six major studios distributed 43 of the top 50 grossing films and 72 of the top 100. Their take was disproportionately large, at 93% of gross in the top 50, and 88% in the top 100.[5] Disney, the dominant studio, had only one theatrical fiction film to gross less than $150 million domestically, and the studio's model reflected the tentpole focus and synergy of recent years.

Independent and specialty distributors have historically played a vital role in documentary distribution in the US. To take a few examples of breakthrough hits (and critical favorites) from the 1980s to the early 2000s, each was distributed by a niche distributor: *The Thin Blue Line* and *Paris is Burning* by Miramax, *Koyaanisqatsi* by Island Alive, *Hoop Dreams* by Fine Line, *Fahrenheit 9/11* and *Grizzly Man* by Lionsgate, *Être et avoir* by New Yorker Films, and *An Inconvenient Truth* by Paramount Vantage.[6] Documentaries formed an important part of these specialty and indie distributors' output, along with indie features, international art cinema, and cult films.[7] The role of documentaries in this distribution sector has, if anything, grown with the theatrical documentary boom of the 2000s and 2010s, and art house theatres regularly program documentaries alongside foreign films and independent fiction films.[8]

Documentaries in 2017 represented a significant portion of distribution at art-house cinemas in the United States. In that year, for instance, the Ritz Landmark Theaters in Philadelphia, an art-house chain, had, on average, two or three documentaries showing out of a dozen or so films at a given time, the rest of the screens dedicated to indie, prestige, and foreign films.[9] While successful in gaining distribution, at least in art house cinemas, documentaries earned far less than the top-performing fiction films and were concentrated in the lower end of the distribution market. By far the most successful documentary of the year was *Born in China*, a Disney nature documentary, with a domestic gross of $13.8 M. Even this film did not fall into the top 100 of the year's box office rankings, and its theatrical run was comparable to a prestige picture like *Jackie* or *Roman J. Israel, Esq.* (though by contrast, some prestige pictures earned four times as much). However, most documentaries earned less than $500,000 in gross receipts in US theaters, and some far less. Unless a documentary was a relative hit, its release tended to be limited to anywhere between 6 and 18 theaters nationwide.

Theatrical box-office returns do not tell the whole story, certainly. Receipts outside the US complicate the picture, though the major studios (historically US-based but now global companies) also have dominance internationally. Also, ancillary distribution across television, home video (physical media or on-demand), and nontheatrical rentals add significantly to a film's revenue. One estimate of *Get Out*, for instance, suggests global television and home entertainment revenues were roughly equal to global theatrical rentals.[10] Hollywood studios have so far weathered the storm of on-demand video with a still robust theatrical return and overall profitability. Like home video before it, on-demand video has been a valuable supplement to the studios' revenue streams.

Beyond the surface success and continuity, though, the rise of digital distribution has transformed film distribution. Economically, it has had a few effects on the distribution marketplace. Release windows (the delays between theatrical, cable TV, and home video releases) have grown shorter, in part because of digital cinema projection in movie theaters, which allows for saturation booking and compression of the theatrical run. Chuck Tryon has argued that digital delivery has transformed moviegoing culture as much as it has offered an alternative to the theatrical experience. As the economic logic of media convergence leads to new technologies of digital delivery, consumers increasingly privilege

the home viewing experience for films.[11] The shift in consumption
cultures has arguably had the strongest impact on independent cinema,
for which distributors sometimes use day–and–date release (simultaneous
theatrical and on–demand). More radically, some subscription video–on–
demand services (SVOD) reserve releases for on–demand distribution
only; since these services get revenue from enticing and keeping sub-
scriptions rather than per film, their focus has been on growing a library
of exclusive titles. As two industry observers describe the recent changes:

> For decades, the traditional order of creating windows of exploita-
> tion of channels of distribution followed a familiar pattern: three to
> six months of theatrical, followed by an educational window, then
> home video and transactional video on demand (TVOD), followed
> by pay TV and then linear TV .... Today, SVOD services often
> want to be day–and–date with TVOD, further truncating windows.
> Clearly, the rate of change is unprecedented, and the level of
> disruption is challenging for distributors and filmmakers alike.[12]

While traditional distribution windows have more shrunk than dis-
appeared, the shifting economics of the major media companies have
prevented a new equilibrium state of distribution from forming.

The market disruption has been especially strong in the area of documentary, as documentary features are likely to get an even bigger portion
of their viewing in the video-on-demand context. Netflix, for one, has
made documentary films and programs mainstays of its service. The reasons
may have to do in part with consumer preference since many documentaries may not be associated with the kind of cinematic spectacle
known to draw audiences for tentpole fiction films. Similarly, while feature
documentaries frequently have a different style and set of production values
than television broadcast documentaries, nonfiction forms have long played
a prominent role in US television programming (and in many other national contexts, too). In this respect, the streaming services are following in
the footsteps of cable television channel HBO, which has long used
documentaries as an important part of their effort to raise the channel's
prestige and gain subscribers.[13] One driving factor, though, is the relatively
low cost for documentary production compared to fiction films. For instance, *Abacus: Too Small to Jail*, about a family-run bank during the fallout
of the 2008 financial crisis, was made on a production budget of
$650,000.[14] By contrast, the mid-budget prestige drama *Manchester by the
Sea* had a production budget of $9 M.[15] Bidding wars can raise the doc-
umentary acquisition costs up considerably (Netflix reportedly paid
$5 million for the exclusive rights to *Icarus*), but the acquisition model

poses much less risk than in-house production since the production companies pay for the production costs and the streaming companies bid on films with strong festival play or audience potential.[16] The services have invested in documentaries but also reserved extensive rights. In 2017, *Icarus, Strong Island,* and *Chasing Coral,* among others, had no regular theatrical release at all; they were exclusively distributed via Netflix.

Theatrical distribution still plays an important role for independent distributors and many independent filmmakers, though. Even if theatrical receipts are not high enough to offset theatrical distribution costs, a theatrical run, however small, can provide a few benefits to the film. It will provide an occasion for popular press reviews and news coverage. It adds to the potential success of the films in home-entertainment formats. Finally, it can boost the profile of the filmmaker.[17] Additionally, Academy Award consideration requires at least a minimal theatrical run. There are three standard approaches to theatrical release: wide (saturation booking at many theaters upon opening), platform (booking only a couple of markets before expanding out slowly) and limited (showing only in markets likely to return publicity).

*Kedi*'s distributor, Oscilloscope, sticks to a theatrical release and distinct window for most of its releases, seeing advantages to the theatrical run and tough challenges in day-and-date releasing. Aaron Katz, director of acquisitions for the company, explains that unlike some distributors with a digital emphasis, Oscilloscope prioritizes the marketing potential of the theatrical release:

> What we've been finding from our successes the past couple years is that when we go theatrically, we're building a real marketing campaign for these films. We're building great press that we wouldn't get if the film was looked at as a digitally-driven title. *The New York Times* doesn't review every movie that's being released now. They only review the ones they think deserve it, and a lot of "day-and-date" titles get lost in that. So our goal is to find good movies and build a profile for them through theatrical release followed by the rest of its releases.[18]

Oscilloscope's approach is not ubiquitous since streaming platforms either release films as digital-only (no theatrical distribution) or digital-driven (minimal theatrical, with day-and-date release), but neither is it unique since distributors going the theatrical route do increasingly see the value for at least a solid limited release.

In the context of the documentary in the distribution landscape of 2017, *Kedi* was an impressive hit at the box office. The documentary was a good example of a film that thrived with a platform rather than a wide release, starting with a small number of theaters in the biggest cities (with influential press coverage) before expanding out as demand grew. It opened at the cinephile and repertory Metrograph cinema in New York and the following week at the Laemmle Royal Theater in Los Angeles; within three weeks, it had expanded to over fifty theaters nationwide and would play in 130 theaters in total in the US.[19] Ultimately, it would gross over $2.8 million from its domestic theatrical release (with a further $2.2 M internationally), an amount that is small compared to successful fiction films but strong for a documentary release. In fact, it was the fourth-highest grossing documentary of the 2017 releases, behind *Born in China*, *I Am Not Your Negro* (another surprise hit), and *An Inconvenient Sequel*. The success was remarkable not only for a non-English language (subtitled) documentary but also one carried by a smaller independent distributor, Oscilloscope, which typically distributes films grossing well under half a million dollars. By comparison, the Oscilloscope release *Brimstone and Glory*, a documentary about fireworks in a rural Mexican town, earned only around $32,000 in US cinemas. *Kedi*'s subscription-VOD distribution was exclusively through the YouTube Premium channel, and library and educational streaming were available for a period through Kanopy.[20] While a platform theatrical release does not always pay the same dividends, Oscilloscope's strategy worked well for *Kedi*.

## Popular art cinema and documentary

The distribution marketplace involves a hierarchical sorting of documentaries by expected earnings potential. Usually, distributors have a good sense of a film's ability to find a market, though there is as much art as science in release strategies. Moreover, films can exceed expectations or fail despite having marketable subject matter and accessible style. While the cutoff between these tiers is not often a stark dividing line, the releases tend to clump together rather than form a steady continuum of performance. These distribution tiers correspond, if imperfectly, to different taste categories. By definition, popular documentaries tend to have a style that appeals broadly so that, for instance, a voiceover narration from a bankable star can help sell a nature documentary to a general audience. On the other end of the distribution spectrum, some documentaries from the film festival circuit will appeal to a small group of cinephiles but break too many documentary conventions to gain much popularity. These taste categories do not have a perfect correspondence to the amount of money a film makes, but different types of documentary do tend to fare differently, based both on distributor expectation and audience response.

I would like to propose a set of critical terms that capture the uneven correspondence between documentary style and industrial hierarchy: the popular documentary, the crossover documentary, the mainstay documentary, and the cinephile documentary. These categories capture the fact that the film industry's approach to distribution is often based on differing expectations of audience tastes. Distributors use their understanding of aesthetic taste to maximize the potential market of a given title. Of these stylistic categories, popular documentary and festival documentary already serve as categories in scholarship, though both remain underexamined.[21] What I call the mainstay is a broad, elastic category, comprising a range of styles dominated by legacy documentary approaches (expository, historical recollective, or character-driven). The taste categories are relatively defined. Popular documentaries avoid the more straightforward and traditional attributes of the mainstay documentaries, crossover documentaries selectively borrow from the popular documentary, and festival documentaries may reject qualities from all the other types (Table 5.1). Certainly, these categories are not always discretely defined, but some version of them underlies distributor decisions and audience expectations.

In the category of very successful films are the popular documentaries, which are the only ones to gross more than $10 million theatrically. These films are often not included within scholars' and film critics' purview of the documentary: nature films, spectacle films (especially IMAX attractions), infotainment films, and high-profile agitprop films.[22] As noted above, the biggest earning nonfiction film for 2017 was *Born in China*, a Disney nature film about Chinese wildlife; it played in over 1,500 theaters and grossed nearly $14 million, a figure far surpassing those of other nonfiction films that year. The nature documentaries typify popular documentary style, using expository voiceover, heavy scoring, and high production values in their visuals. They may use certain cinematographic techniques like time-lapse, drone footage, and macro lens close-ups to achieve a more commercial look. In a different stylistic vein, some agitprop documentaries, of the left and right, from *Fahrenheit 9/11* and *An Inconvenient Truth* to *2016: Obama's America*, have done well enough to be considered popular documentaries. However, in 2017, only *An Inconvenient Sequel* and the creationist film *Is Genesis History?* fit this stylistic category, and their gross was under $5 million, placing them in the next distribution bracket.

The next grouping comprises crossover documentaries, hits that gross between $1 million and $10 million. While these start with a small

*Table 5.1* Distribution categories and example 2017 documentaries

| Distribution category (US theatrical) | Common stylistic traits | Example 2017 documentaries (US theatrical gross $K/ no. of theaters) |
|---|---|---|
| **Popular documentary** (Gross over $10M or over 400 theaters) | Celebrity voiceover Cinematography borrowing elements of spectacle Postproduction effects Heavy scoring | *Born in China* ($13,837K/1,508) *An Inconvenient Sequel* ($3,497K/556) *Is Genesis History?* ($2,570K/704) |
| **Crossover documentary** (Gross between $1M and $10M and over 100 theaters) | Combination of elements from the other categories Synthesis of pictorialism and observational footage Inclusion of subject matter with broad appeal | *I Am Not Your Negro* ($7,124K/320) *The Eagle Huntress* ($3,169K/122) *Kedi* ($2,835K/130) *Jane* ($1,723K/96) *Step* ($1,146K/306) |
| **Mainstay documentary** (Gross between $200K and $1M and over 10 theaters) | Observational or character–driven style Use of social actor testimony as voiceover | *Chasing Trane: The John Coltrane Documentary* ($406K/17) *California Typewriter* ($219K/20) *Bombshell: The Hedy Lamarr Story* ($820K/36) *Obit.* ($315K/22) *Icarus* (N/A) *Joan Didion: The Center Will Not Hold* (N/A) |
| **Cinephile documentary** (Gross under $200K and under 10 theaters) | Formal experimentation Refusal of voiceover narration, or essayistic narration Long–take aesthetic | *Last Men in Aleppo* ($15K/5) *Fire at Sea* ($121K/7) *Karl Marx City* ($41K/4) *No Home Movie* ($33K/5) |

release, they expand to a wide release of at least 100 theaters, sometimes many more. Aesthetically, these films often feature an accessible documentary style and subject matter with broad appeal but less spectacle or agitprop polemic than the popular documentaries. In 2017, there were about ten films in this bracket. *I Am Not Your Negro* adapts the essay film, adding a celebrity voiceover and a faster editing pace, and a strong social-analysis argument. Other films like *Kedi, Jane,* and *The Eagle Huntress* feature animals prominently, even adopting some qualities of the nature documentary. *Step* combines elements of the character-driven and musical documentaries. A critically well-received auteur film like *Faces Places,* with nearly $1 million gross receipts, was on the cusp of this category but has more in common formally with the next bracket.

A range of mainstay documentaries receiving between $100,000 and $1 million in box-office gross receipts follows, films like *Chasing Trane: The John Coltrane Documentary* and *California Typewriter.* These use a platform release for a modest run to anywhere between 25 and 50 theaters; while falling short of the more widely released hits, their distribution sets up a reasonable chance to recoup budgets and even turn a profit. This tier includes a number of musical, biographical, and character-driven documentaries. Stylistically, they rework traditional style (interviews and observational footage) to present their information seamlessly, usually without voiceover narration.[23] As with films like *Bombshell: The Hedy Lamarr Story* and *Obit,* this tier may include subject matter with some marketability to particular demographics but without an immediate appeal to a broad, general audience. While not representing any year's biggest nonfiction hits, the bracket represents a good proportion of documentaries with decent distribution visibility, at least among the theatrically distributed features. Many digitally distributed documentaries like *Icarus* and *Joan Didion: The Center Will Not Hold* fit this category.

Films in the lowest-revenue tier of cinephile documentaries usually receive only a limited release. This bracket includes a number of non-English language documentaries and documentaries from the international film festival circuit, such as *Last Men in Aleppo, Fire at Sea, Karl Marx City,* and *No Home Movie.* Since cinephile documentaries put a premium on formal innovation, they can be stylistically varied. Most play to no more than 10 cinemas, often with the specific purpose of garnering press coverage and awards eligibility. Other than IMAX releases, all documentaries rely extensively on home entertainment revenues (DVD, BluRay, and video on demand), but for this tier especially theatrical distribution often serves as a loss leader for ancillary revenue.

## *Kedi* as crossover documentary

Crossover cinema suggests an appeal across expected industrial categories and audiences. From the point of view of a distributor or industry observer, a film might cross over simply by surpassing the normal distribution expectations, but the crossover film aims for broader success. Sukhmani Khorana defines crossover cinema as its "ability to transgress genre, audience, and cultural borders" and proposes the category as an alternative to transnational theorizations that focus either on popular cinema or art cinema exclusively.[24] This idea taps into a dynamic that theorists of national cinema have pointed out: one path to financial success for a non-Hollywood film is to adopt qualities that will allow for success in Hollywood-dominated markets. Stephen Crofts' category of "imitating Hollywood," for instance, describes crossover attempts of non-Hollywood films to play in the US market.[25] In this light, it is significant that many crossover documentaries are made in non-Anglophone contexts. Whether the crossover film crosses national borders or not, the implication of "crossover" usually implies a film with less marketable aspects (foreign language, art cinema pedigree of auteur, or subcultural subject matter) finding strategies for marketability.

As a crossover documentary, *Kedi* is an excellent example of what Rosalind Galt calls the popular art film. She includes examples like *Amélie* or *City of God* as films that "draw from popular genres but circulate nationally and internationally as prestige productions, linked to the institutions of art cinema."[26] The popular art film, she argues, is not reducible to the middlebrow, but operates between the registers of melodramatic affect and cultural legitimacy. Documentaries do not have many of the formal elements of the popular art films she outlines, but crossover documentaries—that is, documentaries that do not fully count as popular documentaries but include elements to gain wider appeal—are, I argue, the nonfiction version of the popular art film. *Kedi* is self-avowed in its goal of inhabiting an in-between space of the popular art film. In fact, Torun and Wuppermann's production company, Termite Films, states as its mission "a dedication to make genre films that embrace arthouse sensibilities."[27]

The crossover documentary qualifies as popular art cinema on several levels. Formally, it combines elements of popular documentary and more traditional documentary approaches like a character-driven or observational documentary. Thematically, it combines some kind of social analysis with an affective appeal to catharsis and redemption. Discursively, it draws on the cultural capital of the festival circuit and film critics' approbation, yet it also has a crowd-pleasing appeal that goes beyond the normal constituency of cinephilia. Industrially, it receives wide distribution but lacks the audience of the biggest performing nonfiction films. Not all of these traits (formal, thematic, discursive, and industrial) apply to every crossover documentary, but crossover documentaries are defined by the nexus of documentary aesthetics, cultural legitimacy, and distribution strategy.

The recent decade has seen the growth of features that inhabit this in-between space of documentary aesthetics. *The Eagle Huntress* and *Jane* fall into the category, with their reliance on scoring, which shifts away from the underlying narrational approach of observational and archival compilation documentary. Other recent examples include *Honeyland* and *The Summit,* two very different films that both have formal and affective qualities of the popular art film. In practice, the way crossover documentaries borrow from popular cinema varies. *Honeyland* uses editing and shooting style to push the character-driven form to fiction-like seamlessness. *Jane* uses heavy scoring and conventions of the nature documentary. *The Summit* uses commercial postproduction and cinematographic effects to invoke narrative suspense. *The Eagle Huntress* features a voiceover narration from fiction film star Daisy Ridley.

The in-between quality of *Kedi*—half festival film, half popular documentary—informs an aesthetic that straddles stylistic approaches, too. On the surface, it would seem to belong more to the kind of observational documentaries on the festival circuit. *Kedi* lacks voiceover narration and has only two intertitles as a preface:

> Cats have lived in what is now Istanbul for thousands of years. They have seen empires rise and fall and the city shrink and grow. Though cared for by many, they live without a master. And whether adored, despised, or overlooked, they are undeniably a part of everyone's life.

The film's structure proceeds much more like an observational film, building up a larger framework from the editing of footage rather than from an imposition of a clear narrative arc or overarching structure immediately apparent to the spectator. Its alternating structure is constituted through a series of vignettes organized around its feline "characters" and the humans who look after them, including shop owners, artists, and bystanders. Each interview is short, with just a few sentences to anchor the meaning of the segment and contribute to the film's overall theme about the connection between humans and animals and the cats' role in Istanbul's life and identity, whereas the majority of each vignette follows one of the nine featured cats. At times, B-roll footage of the city connects the segments, and at other times montage editing strings together shots of cats in their urban environment. Over the course of the film, sometimes obliquely, the documentary touches on the social and political challenges in Istanbul and in Turkish society, from the role of women to the role of outsiders in the social fabric.

*Kedi*'s cinematography alternates between three styles. The majority of the film is shot in a handheld, observational style. The framing is sometimes more stable, sometimes looser, but a handheld camera marks the interviews, exterior shots of the cats (and their interactions with people), and the B-roll style cityscape footage. Meanwhile, the opening of the film and some transitions use drone aerial footage of the city or slow-motion shots of the cityscape (Figure 5.1). As the documentary proceeds past its expository vignettes, the cinematography shifts to more ground-level shots that follow the cats through city streets and building hallways. Cinematographer Wuppermann used small DSLR cameras on remote-control toy trucks to enable such intimate and dynamic following shots.[28] The effect is akin to the kind of embedded camerawork common to the nature documentary and is a departure from a purely observational style or the locked-down composed look common to many festival documentaries.

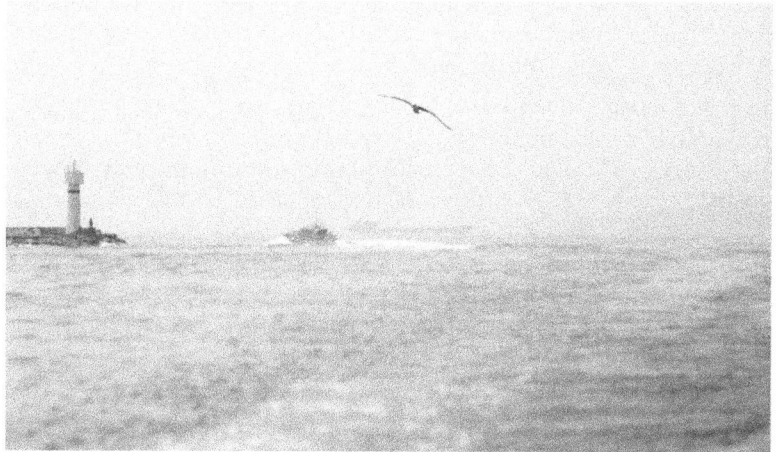

*Figure 5.1* Selective popular-doc style: slow-motion and selective focus in the landscape shot.

The scoring, done by music editor and composer Kira Fontana, involves a combination of approaches too. The opening of the film starts with a moody synthetic string chord over a black screen, and as the dissolve shows the title and opening aerial shot, the recurring theme begins: a Steve Reich-influenced minimalist motif with a vibraphone obligato that develops a playful arpeggio. This minimalist approach (shared by Philip Glass's and Michael Nyman's documentary scores) is a common choice for the crossover documentary, as we see in *Jane,* among many others. In *Kedi,* the scoring alternates with Turkish popular music, particularly pop-rock songs from the 1970s and 1980s with a folk music element or modishness that adds a camp quality today. The first song, "Arkadaşım Eşek," by Barış Manço's group Kurtalan Ekspres, is introduced as the camera style shifts to a more kinetic and playful feel, the song's glockenspiel refrain mimicking the film's score and shifting the emotional tone of the scene. The pop songs add a whimsical tone that cuts against the "discourse of sobriety" that Bill Nichols diagnoses in documentary and that can still define the festival documentary's approach to sound and music.[29]

The structure, a combination of cross-cutting and character-driven arcs, resembles another crossover documentary, 2010s *Babies.* As a composite portrait of four babies (and their families) in Mongolia, Japan, the United States, and Nigeria, *Babies* had certain elements that were putatively observational and other elements that enabled a broader audience appeal. *Kedi* director Torun has noted her fondness for *Babies,* among other films:

> Like *Jiro Dreams of Sushi, Babies, March of the Penguins*; these are films with totally different scales of production value and everything, but all have a common difference from the political issue film …. Really I can only think of four or five in a sea of thousands of these documentaries, and it has been challenging to get this film out into the world because of that reason.[30]

Torun may be overstating the ubiquity of the issue film, but she is responding to a broad sense that most documentaries address political issues as their main objective or as an underlying motif, while these other films avoid or downplay politics. So, despite its formal alliances with festival documentaries, *Kedi,* like popular documentaries, emphasizes universalizing themes and affective content over social and political analysis. In this respect, it is useful to contrast the documentary not only to political documentaries like *An Inconvenient Sequel* but also to pop-culture documentaries like *Amy* and *What Happened Miss Simone?,* which present social analysis (media critique in one, a chronicle of racism in the US in the mid-20th century in the other) as an important part of their structure. There are some political motifs in *Kedi*, but the social analysis is not its main focus.

The relative terrain of taste formations is notable in *Kedi*'s film festival run. The documentary premiered at the Istanbul Film Festival in February 2016 and proceeded to play at a number of festivals, including Full Frame Documentary Festival, Sheffield Doc/Fest, Melbourne International Film Festival, and Vancouver International Film Festival, before its acquisition by Oscilloscope in September 2016.[31] *Kedi* is a film that relied on its festival run to facilitate its ultimate sale. (The filmmakers credit the audience reception at the Seattle International Film Festival for getting interest from distributors.)[32] In the festival ecosystem, *Kedi* played at a mix of festival types, some documentary, some general international festivals, and some thematic. None were top tier festivals like IDFA (International Documentary Festival Amsterdam), Rotterdam, or Berlin; many were festivals that had an international scope and reputation while serving more of a local audience. In the framework of film festival studies, the film played more at audience festivals than at industry festivals (i.e., festivals emphasizing international premieres, film markets, and networking opportunities).[33] After its distributor acquisition and ultimate distribution, it appeared in festivals' non-competition sidebars, such as ZagrebDox's "Happy Dox" program in 2018.[34] Its place in the festival calendar further meant it missed the prominent documentary festivals in the Fall.[35]

*Kedi*, therefore, presents a notable confluence of film festival play and successful theatrical distribution. Film festivals were central to its ultimate distribution plan, yet it relied more on its "audience favorite" reputation than on any set of awards. The initial US-release DVD artwork balances these different audience appeals. The front cover features a cropped version of the movie poster artwork: a photograph of one of the cats in the film and the handwritten "kedi" title (in lower case). Besides a small credit ("a film by Ceyda Torun") and a nearly hidden Oscilloscope logo, the only other design element is a prominent Rotten Tomatoes logo in the corner.[36] The back of the case lists four "official selection" festival accolades and very short pull quotes from critics. In contrast, a more niche festival documentary will foreground both the festival awards and the critics' praise in the promotion. (*Homeland: Iraq Year Zero*'s DVD case is a good example of this practice.) The marketing material cues the expected reading formations for the film, but it also responds to the film's history in the festival circuit and in theaters.[37]

## Conclusion: the indeterminacy of the documentary positioning

*Kedi* shows how the discursive category of the crossover documentary translates into material terms, with box-office returns and digital distribution. As Torun notes of the process of finding distribution, "[W]e were initially rejected by sales agents and the ones that wanted to pick us up would have undersold the film. Had we lost sight of the appeal of our film for audiences, we would have missed out on its success."[38] Torun's comment gets at a complicated truth: structures, from film markets to the taste formations of the festival circuit, are extremely important, but they are not fully determining. Oscilloscope purportedly had faith in the potential appeal of *Kedi* from the start, whereas bigger distributors passed up on a film that ended up being a hit. In retrospect, the documentary does seem to have many elements for crossover success. At the same time, *Kedi* lacked extensive production funds (in contrast with, for instance, *The Act of Killing*, which had Danish Film Institute support), and its festival run showed a modest aspiration, not aiming for (or receiving) the highest festival acclaim or the most extensive pre-distribution promotion. The film's success in hindsight seems apparent, but its path through the media industries was not obvious or automatic.

To position *Kedi* as a crossover documentary, defined in relative terms to other kinds of documentaries, therefore, is useful but also presents challenges. Categories like the crossover documentary help us make sense of an important trend in nonfiction, and they may correspond in part to filmmakers' implicit understanding of the field. However, categories are not tidy entities in themselves. For instance, *I Am Not Your Negro*, a more financially successful film than *Kedi* in 2017, at least in the US, has elements of a popular art film but lacks a recuperative theme. The notion of a popular art film in documentary does not solve all definitional problems, but it usefully suggests a relational aspect to how documentaries style themselves, how they are released, and how they are received. The concept helps us deal with films like *Kedi* that are contradictory and often compelling in their mix of styles and register.

## Notes

1  Arlin Golden, "Interview with KEDI Director Ceyda Torun: 'We All Need To See Things That Remind Us Of The Good Things In The World,'" *Film Inquiry*, February 10, 2017, https://www.filminquiry.com/interview-kedi-director-ceyda-torun/. Unless otherwise relevant to the context, film dates and attribution here are given in the filmography.

2 While the idea of post-cinema usually focuses on theoretical implications of cinema after its move to digital production and exhibition, the term, like "post-network" in television studies, can encompass the post-digital state of cinema in general. See Shane Denson and Julia Leyda, eds., *Post-Cinema; Theorizing Twenty-First Cinema Film* (Falmer: REFRAME Books, 2016). See also, Amanda Lotz, *The Television Will Be Revolutionized* (New York: NYU Press, 2007).

3 Tino Balio, *Hollywood in the New Millennium* (London: British Film Institute, 2013).

4 Geoff King, "Thriving or in Permanent Crisis?: Discourses on the State of Indie Cinema," in *American Independent Cinema: Indie, Indiewood, and Beyond*, eds., Geoff King, Claire Malloy and Yannis Tzioumakis (London: Routledge, 2012), 41–52.

5 Box-office figures, unless otherwise noted, come from the Box Office Mojo website (boxofficemojo.com). While not necessarily perfect as a single source, they provide a good general guide to relative and absolute box-office performance in the United States. Calculations and comparisons in this essay are my own.

6 For more on documentary's navigation of the film industry in the 1980s, see Carl Plantinga, "American Documentary in the 1980s," in *Hollywood under the Electronic Rainbow, 1980–1989*, ed. Stephen Prince (Berkeley: University of California Press, 2002), 370–87.

7 See Yannis Tzioumakis, "'Independent,' 'Indie,' and 'Indiewood': Towards a Periodisation of Contemporary (Post-1980) American Independent Cinema," in *American Independent Cinema*, eds., Geoff King, Claire Malloy and Yannis Tzioumakis (London: Routledge, 2012), 28–40.

8 For an optimistic take on both theatrical and VOD distribution for documentary, see Anthony Kaufman, "Documentary Sales Are Surging, But What's Driving the Competition?" *Indiewire.com*, April 18, 2017, https://www.indiewire.com/2017/04/documentaries-sales-netflix-amazon-hulu-bubble-1201806552/.

9 Assessment based on the Landmark Theaters' promotional emails received in 2017 announcing their weekly releases.

10 Anthony d'Alessandro, "Deadline's 2017 Most Valuable Movie Blockbuster Tournament Gets Underway: No. 10 'Get Out'," *Deadline.com*, March 19, 2018, https://deadline.com/2018/03/get-out-box-office-profit-2017–1202345412/.

11 Chuck Tryon, *On Demand Culture: Digital Delivery and the Future of Movies* (New Brunswick: Rutgers University Press, 2013).

12 Susan Margolin and Jon Reiss, "Independent Documentary Distribution in Turbulent Times," *Documentary Magazine* (Winter 2017), https://www.documentary.org/feature/independent-documentary-distribution-turbulent-times.

13 Gary R. Edgerton and Jeffery P. Jones, eds., *The Essential HBO Reader* (Lexington: University of Kentucky Press, 2008).

14 Barbara Chai, "Oscar-Nominated Documentary Tells Amazing Story of the only U.S. Bank to be Prosecuted after the Financial Crisis," *Marketwatch.com*, March 3, 2018, https://www.marketwatch.com/story/the-story-behind-oscar-nominated-bank-documentary-abacus-small-enough-to-jail-2018-02-27.

15 Sarah Whitten, "Netflix's Disappointing Oscar Night has Some Questioning its Film Strategy," *CNBC.com*, February 16, 2020, https://www.cnbc.com/2020/02/14/oscars-2020-netflixs-disappointing-night-raises-questions-about-strategy.html.

16 Brent Lang, "Sundance: Netflix Lands Russian Doping Documentary 'Icarus'," *Variety*, January 24, 2017, https://variety.com/2017/film/news/sundance-icarus-russian-doping-1201968509/.

17 This list is paraphrased from Bryan Glick of The Film Collaborative, quoted in Margolin and Reiss. For more on the opportunity of filmmaker branding, see Annie Howard, "Lulu Wang Champions A24 Deal for 'The Farewell' Over Streaming Offer," *The Hollywood Reporter,* December 27, 2019, https://www.hollywoodreporter.com/news/lulu-wang-champions-a24-deal-farewell-streaming-offer-director-roundtable-1264206.

18 Jake Brandman, "Behind the Screens: Oscilloscope Laboratories' Underground Movie Model," *Observer.com,* January 13, 2017, https://observer.com/2017/01/behind-the-screens-oscilloscope-laboratories-underground-movie-model/.

19 Kate Erbland, "*Kedi*: How a Documentary About Turkish Street Cats Became a Surprise Box Office Hit," *Indiewire,* April 11, 2017, https://www.indiewire.com/2017/04/kedi-oscilloscpe-documentary-turkish-cats-box-office-1201803669/. On the New York opening weeks, see Jen Carlson, "Beloved Cat Doc *Kedi* Now Screening in Brooklyn & Manhattan," *Gothamist.com,* March 28, 2017, https://gothamist.com/arts-entertainment/beloved-cat-doc-kedi-now-screening-in-brooklyn-manhattan.

20 Todd Spangler, "YouTube Acquires Turkish Street Cats Documentary Film 'Kedi' for YouTube Red," *Variety,* April 20, 2017, https://variety.com/2017/digital/news/youtube-red-kedi-turkish-street-cats-1202391313; Chris O'Fait, "Kanopy: The Free Netflix Alternative Adds 100 Classic Paramount Titles—Exclusive," *Indiewire,* June 6, 2018, https://www.indiewire.com/2018/06/kanopy-free-netflix-alternative-adds-100-classic-paramount-movies-1201971739/.

21 For some scholarly work on these categories, see Angela J. Aguayo, "*Paradise Lost* and Found: Popular Documentary, Collective Identification and Participatory Media Culture," *Studies in Documentary Film* 7, no. 3 (2013): 233–48; and Aida Vallejo, "Documentary Filmmakers on the Circuit: A Festival Career from *A Czech Dream* to a *Czech Peace*," in *Post-1990 Documentary: Reconfiguring Independence,* eds., Camille Deprez and Judith Pernin (Edinburgh: Edinburgh University Press, 2015), 171–87.

22 Scott MacDonald, for instance, laments the scholarly and critical neglect of the nature documentary. "Up Close and Political: Three Short Ruminations on Ideology in the Nature Film," *Film Quarterly* 59, no. 3 (2006): 4–21.

23 The character-driven documentary is a dominant version of this approach, but expository and other documentary types may have a similar streamlining of traditional techniques. For more on this broad approach of documentary narration, see Chris Cagle, "Postclassical Nonfiction: Narration in the Contemporary Documentary," *Cinema Journal* 52, no. 1 (Fall 2012): 45–65.

24 Sukhmani Khorana, "Crossover Cinema: A Genealogical and Conceptual Overview," in *Crossover Cinema: Cross-Cultural Film from Production to Reception,* ed. Sukhmani Khorana (London: Routledge, 2013), 3–13.

25 Stephen Crofts, "Reconceptualizing National Cinema/s," *Quarterly Review of Film and Video* 14, no. 3 (1993): 56.

26 Rosalind Galt, "The Prettiness of Italian Cinema," in *Popular Italian Cinema,* eds., Louis Bayman and Sergio Rigoletto (Basingstoke: Palgrave Macmillan, 2013), 53.

27 "About Termite Films," Termite Films website, accessed March 1, 2020, http://termitefilms.com/about.html.

28 Alissa Simon, "Turkish Helmer's Debut Doc 'Kedi' Tapped for U.S. Release," *Variety,* October 18, 2016, https://variety.com/2016/film/festivals/turkish-helmers-debut-doc-kedi-tapped-for-u-s-release-1201892894/.

29 Bill Nichols, *Representing Reality: Issues and Concepts in Documentary* (Bloomington: Indiana University Press, 1991), 6.

30 Golden, "Interview with KEDI Director Ceyda Torun."

31 Mia Galuppo, "Oscilloscope Lands Cat Doc *Kedi* for North America," *The Hollywood Reporter*, September 22, 2016, https://www.hollywoodreporter.com/news/oscilloscope-lands-cat-doc-kedi-931802. Oscilloscope acquired international rights in the following spring. Leo Barraclough, "Cat Movie *Kedi* Sold to Multiple Countries by Oscilloscope," *Variety*, May 5, 2017, https://variety.com/2017/film/global/1202410224-1202410224/.

32 Golden, "Interview with KEDI Director Ceyda Torun."

33 For the distinction between audience and industry festivals, see Mark Peranson, "First You Get the Power, Then You Get the Money: Two Models of Film Festivals," *Cineaste* 33, no. 3 (2008): 37–43. Reprinted in Richard Porton, ed. *Dekalog 3: On Film Festivals* (London: Wallflower, 2009), 23–37.

34 "Happy Dox," ZagrebDox online program, accessed March 1, 2020, http://zagrebdox.net/en/2018/program/official_program/happy_dox.

35 Erbland, "*Kedi*."

36 Subsequent DVD releases from Oscilloscope have a plainer design without the Rotten Tomatoes tie in. These, including cardboard-package releases, can be read as catering to a more cinephile collector audience.

37 For more on reading formations, see Tony Bennett and Janet Woollacottt, *Bond and Beyond: The Political Career of a Popular Hero* (Houndmills, Basingstoke: Macmillan Education, 1987), 64.

38 Lyra H., "Women Directors: Meet Ceyda Torun—*Kedi,*" Women And Hollywood.com, November 9, 2017, https://womenandhollywood.com/doc-nyc-2017-women-directors-meet-ceyda-torun-kedi-a53c9ed98bc2/.

# Epilogue
## A conversation with *Kedi*'s director, Ceyda Torun

*Kristen Fuhs and Ceyda Torun*

*Kristen Fuhs:*   **When I tell people we're editing a book about *Kedi*, I often say as a follow-up, "you know, the Turkish cat documentary." However, that moniker isn't entirely accurate. The film is set in Istanbul, but it is not "Turkish" by conventional standards of that definition. How do you think about this film in relation to national identity?**

*Ceyda Torun:*   When I describe it, I say "the movie about cats in Istanbul." Our funding came from Germany, the editor is Austrian, the composer is American, the cinematographer is German, another cinematographer is Turkish, the director is Turkish in some ways but not in other ways: it's all a bit of a mixed group of people. The film isn't made entirely by Turks, and it's not made with Turkish money. If we had taken money from the government, we would've had a different set of requirements to fulfill or things to avoid.

I have always found it very strange, these definitions. I understand that the need comes from how festivals are structured, to categorize films in a certain way. But I'm not sure it does justice to the identity of a film, especially those that don't fit the traditional model.

*KF:*   **It's interesting that you specify "Istanbul cats" rather than Turkish cats more broadly. The specificity of Istanbul, rather than another city in Turkey, is important to this film. There's an Istanbul identity that is specific to the city and the story you're telling.**

CT:     Exactly. You could easily make another film about cats in Turkey, and it would feel very different. There would be a lot of segments where you have rural farming towns, and the relationship would be significantly different. Still beautiful, just very, very different. Istanbul is unique in the sense that it's a densely populated city, but it's very different than other highly populated cities. The film wants to show the city as it is, as much as the cats and the people in it. It's the third player in the film.

KF:     **One of the chapters in this book situates *Kedi* as part of a long history of documentaries about Turkey, many of which were made by outsiders who exoticized the location and its people, rarely getting out of the old town or showing anything beyond the Bosphorus and the Hagia Sophia. You were born in Istanbul but moved away when you were 11. Do you think of yourself as an insider or an outsider? What role did your Turkish identity play in how you came to construct this film?**

CT:     I was very aware of wanting to present the city in a way that is markedly different from how complete outsiders or complete insiders of the city would present it, and I think that's why it was important for me to make this film. Moving forward, if I were able to make similar films portrayed through the eyes of other animals (a plan that is on hold right now), I wouldn't direct them myself. I would try to find people like me who have an insider experience of that location with an ability to see it from the outside. That layer of distance allowed me to view the city, the cats, the people, the dynamics in a way that avoided the pitfalls of either being a foreigner or being too close to the subject. We're not the first people to think of wanting to do a documentary with cats in Istanbul. It's just the perspective that was missing. When you're too close to something, you're not able to see what an outsider point of view might value about a subject.

        I was back in Istanbul every summer. My mother made sure that we never lost having Istanbul as part of our identity. I would spend a whole year in New York or Jordan or London and then come back. And my family and I still go back every summer – except for this summer, which really breaks our hearts. It's a perspective that I'm really privileged to have had. When you see the growth of anything, you notice the changes in a much more pronounced way when you haven't been with that thing as it changes.

KF:    **You said once in an interview that you "really wanted to show the world that Istanbul isn't like what we see in news headlines, or a Bond movie or through a tour guide. Capturing the real city was very important to [you]."[1] Why are cats a good interlocutor for discovering the "real" Istanbul?**

CT:    Cats have this ability to move across and within divides, whether it's socioeconomic divides, educational divides, or divides between men and women. They have access to an experience of being present in a place in a much more flexible and open way than humans do. These cats know their neighborhood in a way that human beings would never know because they're not using them in the same way. The cat knows exactly where that hole is in the fence so she can make a quick escape. It's a hole that you've never noticed, and you've lived there for 20 years in that very spot. You eat lunch there every day and you've never noticed that spot because you never had to think about using it.

I wanted to physically film from the perspective of the cats as much as possible. We discovered that it was too intrusive to try to get a camera on the cat. We tried to get one of those cat harnesses, which we thought we could equip with a GoPro or a mini camera. We explored a lot of options, but that defeated the purpose of what I wanted to achieve. I wanted to make a film that was respectful to the cat but putting a harness and a camera on it is disrespectful.

KF:    **Another chapter in this book calls *Kedi* a "requiem" for a disappearing, multi-species community. Yet, I've seen you describe this film elsewhere as "childish in many ways, in its optimism."[2] One thing that strikes me as I watch the film is how invested people are in their neighborhood cats—they**

Epilogue 89

don't just passively interact with them, they know about births, deaths, fights, power struggles. They know the cats—and gossip about them—as they would any other neighbor. I, too, find the sense of community and shared responsibility on display here optimistic. And yet, I can't help mourning the lack of this in my own community or the sense that this way of life is disappearing in Istanbul. Can the film be both hopeful and a requiem at the same time?

CT: It is possible that something can be hopeful and a little sad at the same time. What motivates us to want to preserve something or to become aware of its fragility? If somebody had made this film when I was a kid, the city's changes would have been even more pronounced. My mom describes her childhood in a way that is very idyllic: she had 14 acres of trees to run through. When I was a kid, I had 3 fruit trees in the backyard of our apartment building. Now, my sister's kids don't even have a backyard. It has little to do with money and everything to do with accessibility: there just isn't enough space for everyone.

There is something melancholic or nostalgic about the idea that things are changing, but at the same time, things will always change. I think a very powerful effect that a film like this can have is to make you question your desire for an experience of community like this. Once you recognize that desire, you can create the opportunity for it to happen. If it's not about cats, it's something else. The cat thing in Istanbul is unique and incredibly special, and that's why I wanted to make sure there was some kind of documentation of it. Because it will undoubtedly change in another 20 years. It may not disappear, but it will be different. Maybe being both hopeful and a little bit sad at the same time is just the way we experience everything in life. Nothing really stays exactly the same, and we must use it as a way to pay attention to the things that are dear to us.

KF: The first two chapters of this book place *Kedi* alongside other recent documentaries about animals—*Sweetgrass, Nénette, Leviathan, Bestiaire,* and *Taşkafa, Stories of the Street*—as films that, unlike the *National Geographic* or *Planet Earth* documentaries,

**are invested in representing animals as agential beings. I've read that you considered a sort of** *March of the Penguins* **model in the initial stages of pre-production but quickly jettisoned that idea. Were you inspired by other documentaries about animals in your approach to this film?**

CT:     I haven't seen all of those films, but I've seen some of them. In *Nénette*, you have a captive animal that is definitely not where she should be, and it's really a study of how we feel about that. With *Sweetgrass*, it's a livestock animal, and I don't think it's so much about the animals as it is about the humans. Any animal that we've manipulated to the point of being our food source, we've already changed them from their natural selves. I don't know to what extent that animal is authentically that animal anymore. In *Kedi*, I wanted to present the natural state of these cats, which is why you don't see any altered breeds in the film. The street cat you see in *Kedi* is the cat that developed 10,000 years ago in that region. It's more like studying a native animal that happened to be there evolving with humans, rather than evolved by humans.

It was difficult to find films about animals that we wanted to model the film after because you're right: it's either a very big, $10+ million budget film that is gorgeously shot with a 100 person crew, or it's very arthouse, very abstract, very 'I'm just going to put a camera here and you guys make sense of what you're seeing.' We were actually inspired a lot by *Babies*, which has a nice balance of being suggestive with the footage but at the same time trying to be as uninterested as possible in the dynamics of what was being filmed. Documentaries are put into categories that make it easier for salespeople and distributors to figure out how to get them to audiences, so we kind of had to make up what the film could be. Charlie (my husband, producing partner, and cinematographer) and I—our experience is in fiction filmmaking, this is the first documentary we ever made. Logistically speaking, we didn't know how else to approach it, but in the way we would approach a fiction film, in terms of quantifying the amount of prep work and shooting time in order to get it done and out into the world in a certain time frame. My idea of breaking it up into segments was in part influenced by that need, but at the same time, it created that style of emulating a cat-like philosophy of fluidly moving along from thing to thing.

KF: **It's interesting to hear that the way you structured the film is both a product of narrative decisions related to how best to tell these cats' stories and also business decisions connected to how you would sell this story to the marketplace.**

CT: Yes, and also business decisions in the sense that I knew I didn't want to spend 10 years making a documentary about this. In the documentary world, it's often the case that you're stuck making a project for years and years. I didn't want to make it political. I didn't want to make it specific to any one time frame, even though there are clues in the film for someone who knows. But the significance of when it was filmed is not relevant to the overall experience of the film for me. Or at least that's how I wanted to construct it. You can make a highly politicized film with cats and the politics of Turkey, but I wouldn't know how to do that, to be perfectly honest.

KF: **Did you ever consider taking a more political approach that rooted this story in its specific time?**

CT: Let me tell you how this film came to be and what was happening in Istanbul at the time. The summer of 2013 was the Gezi Park protests that erupted out of the government wanting to build a mall on the last piece of green space in Taksim Square, which was populated by thousand-year-old trees. They started the process without it being a democratic decision: it was more like, 'we're just going to do this,' and some idiot is going to start bulldozing trees. So, the impetus for that protest was for the community to try to hold on to something that is a part of their identity and their philosophy of preservation and investment into authentic things. A mall is not a long-term investment in the culture or the lifestyle of a community. An opera house might be, but a mall isn't.

We arrived for our 2-week trial shoot that summer. We literally landed in Istanbul the night that they set fires to the tents of peaceful protesters, and we were staying down the street from the protests. I had been in contact with my friends who were all there, and until that moment, it was like a festival vibe. But suddenly it turned from that into 'Oh my god, they're killing people over this' and us trying to figure out in that tear-gas environment what we're making with this film and what it all means. I cautiously avoided getting into politics because politics is very divisive. I knew that when I was talking to someone, if we had decided in advance that we didn't align politically, then we could never talk about cats. And the beautiful thing about talking about cats is that it allows you to have a conversation with someone that you may not have otherwise engaged in conversation with, either because of ideological differences or because your worlds don't otherwise collide. You can have conversations with people about cats that have nothing to do with politics or religion or ideology, and therefore it's a beautiful way to connect.

So, when we returned the following summer in 2014 to actually film these cats, it was a summer of calm. The Gezi protests were done. The building of the mall was stopped. Everyone had a sense of accomplishment. But, at the same time, there was a lingering feeling of impending doom, even though it seemed like it was fine, like it was under control. And that's when we actually filmed the people and the cats. We occasionally got into conversations about politics, but nobody really knew what was to come.

At the time we were filming, I didn't understand the ramifications of what we were experiencing. I knew that if I included politics, I ran the risk of misinterpreting or misrepresenting it and tainting the experience of the cats. It's one thing to make a film about politics, but then it becomes journalistic. It becomes reporting, which is fine—you want to have live reporting of incidents without having to make commentary about them, without having to draw conclusions. But when you're making a film that you then go and edit over a long period of time, you are making statements. And if you're not clear about what those statements might be, I think it's very dangerous, in the sense that you might do injustice to things. It's a big responsibility that I don't think anyone should take very lightly, that I don't take very lightly.

KF: **Let's shift gears a bit and talk about the soundtrack: I think the soundscape is one of the most memorable aspects of this documentary. One of the chapters in the book describes *Kedi*'s Istanbul as sounding like the Istanbul of your childhood. How did you conceive of the sound design for the film?**

CT: I appreciate that you brought this up. Because of the score and the songs, different audiences will experience the film differently. It's almost a private nod to the Turkish audience. Honestly, you could put subtitles under a song's lyrics, and it will never have the same effect it does if you're hearing it in its original language. I felt absolutely no need to try to get the foreign audience to understand. A certain song is not going to evoke the same emotional response in someone who never heard the song before as for someone who grew up with it.

I was very conscious of trying to collect iconic songs that represented a certain era, but there are also a couple of songs that are timeless. The Eartha Kitt rendition of "Uska Dara" is a song etched in the memories of pretty much every Turk over the age of 30. I wanted to find songs that either foreigners had made of Turkish music or Turkish songs that had some Western influence. I wanted to highlight those songs because Istanbul is very much a place where different influences create new things. These songs would never exist in the way that they do if they weren't influenced by both sides. Eartha Kitt would never have done "Uska Dara" if she hadn't come to Istanbul or been influenced by Istanbul.

I worked with our composer Kira Fontana on the score. At some point, she wanted to experiment with more Eastern sounds, but I was very keen that I didn't want that stereotypical soundscape. I didn't want to make anyone feel like the music cue was telling them they were watching a film about Turkey. These cats might be living in what is now Turkey, but I don't consider them Turkish. They're just cats. So, in many ways, the score tries to emulate the fleet-footedness of cats. There's something delicate about their movement. When you're moving through the city in the film, which is when you hear the score, you're moving like them.

KF:    **Can you talk about the challenges you had in selling this concept—and the final film—to a fickle marketplace? How important was the festival circuit for you?**

CT:    We are not documentary filmmakers with a catalog of films, so we were coming into this as complete unknowns to the people who were going to potentially buy and sell this film. We reached out to a lot of sales agents, and pretty much the immediate response was, 'We don't know how to sell this film, but we can put it in our catalog and take it to the markets and see how it goes.' We didn't think anyone was going to get *Kedi* from a tiny blurb in a catalog, so we didn't want to risk it.

Then we got into Salem Film Festival. I have to give them props because they were the first ones to respond to the film. And the film is so appropriate for Salem! Immediately after Salem, we had a wonderful reception at Full Frame, and then Seattle Film Festival was where the film really broke out. The biggest lesson we learned from our festival experience is that you shouldn't make assumptions about which festivals you think are right for your film. With Seattle—maybe because it's kind of similar to Istanbul in the sense that it's a port town, they're liberal, they're open to the world, there are a lot of academics—for whatever reason, people were lining up around the block with cat ears on, waiting to get into the film. It was the response of the attendees at Seattle Film Festival that got the attention of two distributors, one of whom was Oscilloscope. We saw eye to eye with them on how to proceed with the film: we knew we had to have a theatrical release because the communal experience of this film is so cool. Like a horror movie you want to see with a bunch of other people so you're all shouting at the same thing, with *Kedi*, it's everyone at the same time going "awwww." It was such a sweet experience that we knew we had to try for a theatrical run. Luckily, Oscilloscope believed in the film's potential and was very,

very smart in their strategy for releasing it. They were able to give it the attention it needed and knew the right way to market it, but I was still genuinely surprised by its success. A lot of sales agents that we had been in touch with wrote again and said they regretted turning us away.

KF:    **One of the book's chapters actually speaks to this. In hindsight, the film's success seems apparent. You've got this great subject, a heartwarming story, beautiful visuals—the package all comes together. So, you look at it and think: of course this movie did well at the box office, of course it found an audience. But the path isn't obvious when you're starting from the beginning and you're trying to convince people you've got something.**

CT:    Absolutely. You have to remind yourself to be flexible and adjust to what feedback you're getting without letting go of your convictions. We could've given the film to a sales agent and ended up in their catalog, and had we had greater time pressure to deliver a financial return on the film, we might have had to choose that option. Going into documentaries, we thought that there was a bigger range or a bigger opportunity to be more experimental with films, but we found that the documentary world is not much different than the world of narrative film. It's also a business in the end. Nonetheless, the fact that a little film like *Kedi* can make it to a global audience is incredibly reassuring.

*This interview was edited and condensed for length and clarity.*

## Notes

1 Kathryn Bromwich, "I Made a Love Letter to the City and the Cats," *The Guardian*, June 18, 2017, https://www.theguardian.com/lifeandstyle/2017/jun/18/kedi-film-istanbul-street-cats.
2 Dalton DeStefano, "Kedi: Review and an Interview with Director Ceyda Torun," 34st.com, March 14, 2017, https://www.34st.com/article/2017/03/keid-a-review-and-interview-with-directors.

# Bibliography

Açar, Mehmet. "Roman, Müze ve Film." *Habertürk*. March 27, 2016. https://www.haberturk.com/yazarlar/mehmet-acar/1215784-roman-muze-ve-film.

Adam, Carol. *The Sexual Politics of Meat: A Feminist Vegetarian Critical Theory*. New York: Continuum, 1999.

Aguayo, Angela J. "*Paradise Lost* and Found: Popular Documentary, Collective Identification and Participatory Media Culture." *Studies in Documentary Film* 7, no. 3 (2013): 233–248.

Alemdar, Melis. "Hit Film about Istanbul's Cats Finally Comes Home to Turkey." https://www.trtworld.com/magazine/hit-film-about-istanbul-s-cats-finally-comes-home-to-turkey-7498.

"Andrea Luka Zimmerman in Conversation with Lucy Reynolds: Chelsea College of Arts, London." *Moving Image Review & Art Journal* (November 19, 2014): 230–245.

Arslan, Savaş. *Cinema in Turkey: A New Critical History*. Oxford: Oxford University Press, 2011.

Aydemir, Şenay. "Mumya: Ölüyle Şaka Olmaz! – Şenay Aydemir." *Duvar*, June 9, 2017. https://www.gazeteduvar.com.tr/yazarlar/2017/06/09/mumya-oluyle-saka-olmaz/.

Aytekin, Deniz. "Amerika'da Gişe Rekorları Kıran Kedi Filmi Bugün Vizyona Giriyor." *Yeşilist*, June 9, 2017. https://www.yesilist.com/amerikada-gise-rekorlari-kiran-kedi-filmi-bugun-vizyona-giriyor/.

Aytekin, Hakan. "Belgesel Sinemamıza 'Milat' Seçmek." In *Belgesel Sinema 2009–2010*, edited by Hakan Aytekin. Istanbul: Belgesel Sinemacılar Birliği, 2011.

Aytekin, Hakan. *Türkiyede Toplumsal Değişme ve Belgesel Sinema*. Istanbul: Belgesel Sinemacılar Birliği, 2016.

Balan, Canan. "Wondrous Pictures in Istanbul: From Cosmopolitanism to Nationalism." In *Early Cinema and the "National"*, edited by Richard Abel, Giorgio Bertellini, and Rob King, 170–182. Herts: John Libbey Publishing, 2008.

Balio, Tino. *Hollywood in the New Millennium*. London: British Film Institute, 2013.

Ban, Sonay. "From Urban Politics to the Politics of Representation: Representing Istanbul's Urban Transformation in Urban Activism Documentaries of the 2000s." *Sabancı University*, 2012. http://research.sabanciuniv.edu/24130/1/SonayBan_443397.pdf.

Barraclough, Leo. "Cat Movie *Kedi* Sold to Multiple Countries by Oscilloscope." *Variety*, May 5, 2017. https://variety.com/2017/film/lobal/1202410224-1202410224/.

Batuman, Bülent. "City, Image, Nation: Ankara, The Heart of Turkey and the Making of National Subjects." In *Cities in Film: Architecture, Urban Space and the Moving Image*, edited by J. Halam, R. Koeck, R. Kronenburg, and L. Roberts, 7–15. Liverpool: University of Liverpool and Arts & Humanities Research Council, 2008.

Bayraktaroğlu, Kerem. "A Question of Identity in Turkish Film: The 45th Antalya Film Festival." *Indiewire*, October 21, 2008. https://www.indiewire.com/2008/10/dispatch-from-turkey-a-question-of-identity-in-turkish-film-the-45th-antalya-film-festival-and-4t-71536/.

Behlil, Melis, and Esin Paca Cengiz. "Selections from the Fight for National Cinema, by Halit Refiğ." *Cinema Journal 55*, no. 3 (2016): 1–16.

Bennett, Tony, and Janet Woollacottt. *Bond and Beyond: The Political Career of a Popular Hero*. Houndmills, Basingstoke: Macmillan Education, 1987.

Berger, John. *"Review of John Berger's"King: A Street Story*. New York: Pantheon, 1999.

Bergfelder, Tim. "National, Transnational or Supranational Cinema? Rethinking European Film Studies." *Media, Culture & Society 27*, no. 3 (2005): 315–331.

Bousé, Derek. "False Intimacy: Close-ups and Viewer Involvement in Wildlife Films." *Visual Studies 18*, no. 2 (2003): 123–132.

Brandman, Jake. "Behind the Screens: Oscilloscope Laboratories' Underground Movie Model." *Observer.com*, January 13, 2017. https://observer.com/2017/01/behind-the-screens-oscilloscope-laboratories-underground-movie-model/.

Bromwich, Kathryn. "I Made a Love Letter to the City and the Cats." *The Guardian*, June 18, 2017. https://www.theguardian.com/lifeandstyle/2017/jun/18/kedi-film-istanbul-street-cats.

Cagle, Chris. "Postclassical Nonfiction: Narration in the Contemporary Documentary." *Cinema Journal 52*, no. 1 (Fall 2012): 45–65.

Candan, Can. "Documentary Cinema in Turkey: A Brief Survey of the Past and the Present." In *The City in Turkish Cinema*, edited by Hakkı Başgüney and Özge Özdüzen, 113–134. Istanbul: Libra Kitap, 2014.

Candan, Can. *"Kültür Filmleri."* *Altyazı*, June 2010.

Carlson, Jen. "Beloved Cat Doc *Kedi* Now Screening in Brooklyn & Manhattan." *Gothamist.com*, March 28, 2017. https://gothamist.com/arts-entertainment/beloved-cat-doc-kedi-now-screening-in-brooklyn-manhattan.

Castaing-Taylor, Lucien. "Iconophobia." *Transition 6*, no. 69 (1996): 64–88.

Ceylan, Tülün Seyhan. "Policies of Turkish Radio Television Corporation (TRT): The Case of the Directorate of Documentary Programs." *Middle East Technical University*, 2006. http://etd.lib.metu.edu.tr/upload/3/12607297/index.pdf.

Chai, Barbara. "Oscar-Nominated Documentary Tells Amazing Story of the only U.S. Bank to be Prosecuted after the Financial Crisis." *Marketwatch.com*, March 3, 2018. https://www.marketwatch.com/story/the-story-behind-oscar-nominated-bank-documentary-abacus-small-enough-to-jail-2018-02-27.

Chaudhuri, Una. *Animal Acts: Performing Species Today*. Ann Arbor, MI: University of Michigan Press, 2014.

Chaudhuri, Una. "(De)Facing the Animals: Zooësis and Performance." *TDR: The Drama Review 51*, no. 1 (Spring 2007): 8–20.

Cowan, Jane K. "Fixing National Subjects in the 1920s Southern Balkans: Also an International Practice." *American Ethnologist 35*, no. 2 (May 1, 2008): 338–356.

Crofts, Stephen. "Reconceptualizing National Cinema/s." *Quarterly Review of Film and Video 14*, no. 3 (1993): 49–67.

d'Alessandro, Anthony. "Deadline's 2017 Most Valuable Movie Blockbuster Tournament Gets Underway: No. 10 'Get Out'." *Deadline.com*, March 19, 2018. https://deadline.com/2018/03/get-out-box-office-profit-2017-1202345412/.

Daniher, Colleen Kim. "Yella Gal: Eartha Kitt's Racial Modulations." *Women & Performance: A Journal of Feminist Theory 28*, no. 1 (2018): 16–33.

Deleuze, Gilles, and Félix Guattari. *A Thousand Plateaus: Capitalism and Schizophrenia*, trans. Brian Massumi. Minneapolis, MN: University of Minnesota Press, 1987.

Denson, Shane, and Julia Leyda, eds. *Post-Cinema: Theorizing Twenty-First Century Film*. Falmer: REFRAME Books, 2016.

Derrida, Jacques. "The Animal That Therefore I Am (More to Follow)." *Critical Inquiry 28*, no. 2 (2002): 369–418.

Eaton, Rebecca M. Doran. "Marking Minimalism: Minimal Music as Sign of Machines and Mathematics in Multimedia." *Music and the Moving Image 7*, no.1 (Spring 2014): 3–23.

Edgerton, Gary R., and Jeffery P. Jones, eds. *The Essential HBO Reader*. Lexington: University of Kentucky Press, 2008.

Egoyan, Atom, and Ian Balfour. "Introduction." In *Subtitles: On the Foreignness of Film*, edited by Atom Egoyan and Ian Balfour, 21–30. Cambridge, MA: MIT Press, 2004.

Eldem, Edhem. "Istanbul as a Cosmopolitan City." In *A Companion to Diaspora and Transnationalism*, edited by Ato Quayson and Girish Daswani, 212–245. West Sussex: Wiley Blackwell, 2013.

Elsaesser, Thomas. *European Cinema: Face to Face with Hollywood*. Amsterdam: Amsterdam University Press, 2005.

Erbland, Kate. "*Kedi*: How a Documentary About Turkish Street Cats Became a Surprise Box Office Hit." *Indiewire*, April 11, 2017. https://www.indiewire.com/2017/04/kedi-oscilloscpe-documentary-turkish-cats-box-office-1201803669/.

Erdoğan, Nezih. "The Spectator in the Making: Modernity and Cinema in Istanbul, 1896–1928." In *Orienting Istanbul: Cultural Capital of Europe?* edited by Deniz Göktürk, Levent Soysal, and Ipek Tureli, 145–159. Oxfordshire & New York: Routledge, 2010.

Ergun, Levent. "The Golden Microphone as a Moment of Hegemony." In *Made in Turkey: Studies in Popular Music*, edited by Ali C. Gedik, 75–88. New York: Routledge, 2018.

Evered, Kyle T. "Symbolizing a Modern Anatolia: Ankara as Capital in Turkey's Early Republican Landscape." *Comparative Studies of South Asia, Africa and the Middle East 28*, no. 2 (2008): 326–341.

Evren, Burçak. *Sigmund Weinberg: Türkiye'ye Sinemayı Getiren Adam*. Istanbul: Milliyet Yayınları, 1995.

"Film-Makers Withdraw from Istanbul Festival in Censorship Protest." *The Guardian*, April 13, 2015. https://www.theguardian.com/world/2015/apr/13/film-makers-withdraw-films-istanbul-film-festival.

Foucault, Michel. *The Will to Knowledge: The History of Sexuality Vol. 1 (originally published in 1976)*, trans. Robert Hurley. London: Penguin Books, 1998.

Foucault, Michel. *"Society Must be Defended" Lectures at the Collège de France, 1975-76*, trans. David Macey. New York: Picador, 2003.

Frase, Brigitte. *"King: A Street Story."* *New York Times Book Reviews* (June 13, 1999): 1.

Frith, Simon. *Performing Rites: On the Value of Popular Music*. Cambridge, MA: Harvard University Press, 1998.

Fudge, Erica. *Pets*. London and New York: Routledge, 2014.

Galt, Rosalind. "The Prettiness of Italian Cinema." In *Popular Italian Cinema*, edited by Louis Bayman and Sergio Rigoletto, 52–68. Basingstoke: Palgrave Macmillan, 2013.

Galt, Rosalind. "Cats and the Moving Image: Feline Cinematicity from Lumiere to Maru." In *Animal Life and the Moving Image*, edited by Michael Lawrence and Laura McMahon. London; New York: Palgrave, on behalf of the British Film Institute, 2015.

Galuppo, Mia. "Oscilloscope Lands Cat Doc *Kedi* for North America." *The Hollywood Reporter*, September 22, 2016. https://www.hollywoodreporter.com/news/oscilloscope-lands-cat-doc-kedi-931802.

Golden, Arlin. "Interview With KEDI Director Ceyda Torun: 'We All Need To See Things That Remind Us Of The Good Things In The World'." *Film Inquiry*, February 10, 2017. https://www.filminquiry.com/interview-kedi-director-ceyda-torun/.

Graham, Latria. "Eartha Kitt, Coming Home." *Oxford American 21*, no.107 (Winter 2019): 42–48.

Gültekin, Setenay. "Turkish Psychedelia: The Revival of Anatolian Pop." *Kadir Has University*, 2019. http://academicrepository.khas.edu.tr/bitstream/handle/20.500.12469/2771/Turkishpsychedelia therevivalofAnatolianpop.pdf?sequence=1&isAllowed=y.

Gurata, Ahmet. "City of Intrigues. Istanbul as an Exotic Attraction." In *World Film Locations: Istanbul*, edited by Özlem Köksal, 24–41. Bristol: Intellect Books, 2012.

H., Lyra. "DOC NYC 2017 Women Directors: Meet Ceyda Torun – 'Kedi'." https://womenandhollywood.com/doc-nyc-2017-women-directors-meet-ceyda-torun-kedi-a53c9ed98bc2/.

Haraway, Donna Jeanne. "Crittercam: Compounding Eyes in Naturecultures." In *When Species Meet. Posthumanities 3*. Minneapolis: University of Minnesota Press, 2008.

Haraway, Donna Jeanne. "Anthropocene, Capitalocene, Plantationocene, Chthulucene: Making Kin." *Environmental Humanities 6* (2015): 159–165.

Hersh, Seymour. "C.I.A. in '68 Gave Secret Service a Report Containing Gossip About Eartha Kitt After White House Incident." *New York Times*, January 3, 1975. https://www.nytimes.com/1975/01/03/archives/cia-in-68-gave-secret-service-a-report-containing-gossip-about.html.

Higson, Andrew. "The Concept of National Cinema." *Screen 30*, no. 4 (1989): 36–47.

Higson, Andrew. "The Limiting Imagination of National Cinema." In *Cinema and Nation*, edited by Mette Hjort and Scott MacKenzie, 63–74. London and New York: Routledge, 2000.

Howard, Annie. "Lulu Wang Champions A24 Deal for 'The Farewell' Over Streaming Offer." *The Hollywood Reporter*, December 27, 2019. https://www.hollywoodreporter.com/news/lulu-wang-champions-a24-deal-farewell-streaming-offer-director-roundtable-1264206.

Hubbert, Julie. "The Compilation Soundtrack from the 1960s to the Present." In *The Oxford Handbook of Film Music Studies*, edited by David Neumeyer, 291–318. New York: Oxford, 2013.

Hullfish, Steve. "AOTC with editor of the documentary 'KEDI.' https://www.providecocoalition.com/aotc-kedi/.

Ingram, David. *Green Screen: Environmentalism and Hollywood Cinema. Representing American Culture*. Exeter: University of Exeter Press, 2004.

Isler, Hilal. "The Surprising Story of Eartha Kitt in Istanbul." *The Paris Review*, October 1, 2018. https://www.theparisreview.org/blog/2018/10/01/eartha-kitt-in-istanbul/.

"İstanbul Municipality Closes Magazine Due to Cat Photo." *bianet.org*, 2017. http://bianet.org/english/freedom-of-expression/186510-istanbul-municipality-closes-magazine-due-to-cat-photo?bia_source=rss.

Kaplan, E. Ann. *Climate Trauma: Foreseeing the Future in Dystopian Film and Fiction*. New Brunswick, NJ: Rutgers University Press, 2016.

Kara, Fatih, and Ismail Yucel. "Climate Change Effects on Extreme Flows of Water Supply Area in Istanbul: Utility of Regional Climate Models and Downscaling Method." *Environmental Monitoring and Assessment 187*, no. 9 (August 22, 2015): 580.

Kara, Mesut. "Sinematek ve Genç Sinema Hareketi." *Evrensel*, April 6, 2013. https://www.evrensel.net/yazi/53522/sinematek-ve-genc-sinema-hareketi.

Karpat, Kemal H. "The People's Houses in Turkey: Establishment and Growth." *Middle East Journal 17*, no. 1/2 (1963): 55–67.

Kaufman, Anthony. "Documentary Sales Are Surging, But What's Driving the Competition?" *Indiewire.com*, April 18, 2017. https://www.indiewire.com/2017/04/documentaries-sales-netflix-amazon-hulu-bubble-1201806552/.

Kaya, Dilek. "Remembering the First Movie Theaters and Early Cinema Exhibition in Quay, Smyrna, Turkey." In *The Routledge Companion to New Cinema History*, edited by Daniel Biltereyst, Richard Maltby, and Phillippe Meers, 244–253. London and New York: Routledge, 2019.

Kaya Mutlu, Dilek. "The Russian Monument at Ayastefanos (San Stefano): Between Defeat and Revenge, Remembering and Forgetting." *Middle Eastern Studies 43*, no. 1 (January 2007): 75–86.

"Kedi – Box Office Türkiye." https://boxofficeturkiye.com/film/kedi-2013541.

KEDI Press kit. https://www.dropbox.com/sh/5vyuub2vr764uc7/AABV1NpXd-sfTYz3qEWRFx0da?dl=0.

Kenny, Glenn. "Cute Cats of 'Kedi,' Rekindling a 'Love of Life'." *New York Times*, February 9, 2017. https://www.nytimes.com/2017/02/09/movies/kedi-review.html.

Khorana, Sukhmani. "Crossover Cinema: A Genealogical and Conceptual Overview." In *Crossover Cinema: Cross-Cultural Film from Production to Reception*, edited by Sukhmani Khorana, 3–13. London: Routledge, 2013.

King, Geoff. "Thriving or In Permanent Crisis?: Discourses on the State of Indie Cinema." In *American Independent Cinema: Indie, Indiewood, and Beyond*, edited by Geoff King, Claire Malloy, and Yannis Tzioumakis, 41–52. London: Routledge, 2012.

Kirksey, S. Eben, and Stefan Helmreich. "The Emergence of Multispecies Ethnography." *Cultural Anthropology 25*, no. 4 (2010): 545–576.

Kitt, Eartha. *Thursday's Child*. New York: Duell, Sloan and Pearce, 1956.

Kitt, Eartha. *Alone with Me: A New Autobiography*. Chicago: Henry Regnery, 1976.

Kitt, Eartha. *Confessions of a Sex Kitten*. Fort Lee, NJ: Barricade, 1989.

"Kitty Cam: The Project Attaching Cameras to Cats as They Move through the Wild." https://slate.com/news-and-politics/2012/08/kitty-cam-the-project-attaching-cameras-to-cats-as-they-move-through-the-wild.html.

"'KittyCam' Reveals High Levels of Wildlife Being Killed by Outdoor Cats." *American Bird Conservancy*. https://abcbirds.org/article/kittycam-reveals-high-levels-of-wildlife-being-killed-by-outdoor-cats/.

Kural, Nil. "Kayıp İstanbul'un Izindeki Belgesel." *Milliyet*, March 12, 2016. https://www.milliyet.com.tr/yazarlar/nil-kural/kayip-istanbul-un-izindeki-belgesel-2208208.

Ladino, Jennifer. "For the Love of Nature: Documenting Life, Death, and Animality in *Grizzly Man* and *March of the Penguins*." *Interdisciplinary Studies in Literature and Environment 16*, no. 1 (Winter 2009): 53–90.

Lang, Brent. "Sundance: Netflix Lands Russian Doping Documentary 'Icarus'." *Variety*, 24 January, 2017. https://variety.com/2017/film/news/sundance-icarus-russian-doping-1201968509/.

Lawrence, Michael, and Laura McMahon. *Animal Life and the Moving Image*. London; New York: Palgrave, on behalf of the British Film Institute, 2015.

Leopold, Aldo. *A Sand County Almanac & Other Writings on Ecology and Conservation. Special Commemorative Ed. Library of America 238*. New York: Library of America, 2013.

Lotz, Amanda. *The Television Will Be Revolutionized*. New York: NYU Press, 2007.

Luke, Timothy W. "On Environmentality: Geo-Power and Eco-Knowledge in the Discourses of Contemporary Environmentalism." *Cultural Critique 31* (Autumn, 1995): 57–81.

MacDonald, Scott. "Up Close and Political: Three Short Ruminations on Ideology in the Nature Film." *Film Quarterly 59*, no 3 (2006): 4–21.

Margolin, Susan, and Jon Reiss, "Independent Documentary Distribution in Turbulent Times." *Documentary Magazine* (Winter 2017). https://www.documentary.org/feature/independent-documentary-distribution-turbulent-times.

Marra, Peter P. *Cat Wars: The Devastating Consequences of a Cuddly Killer*. Princeton: Princeton University Press, 2016.

Matharu, Priya. "Crazy Kedi Ladies and Gentlemen, Just for You, an Interview with Kira Fontana." http://magazine.scoreit.org/crazy-kedi-ladies-gentlemen-just-interview-kira-fontana/.

McKinney, Michael L. "Urbanization as a Major Cause of Biotic Homogenization." *Biological Conservation 127*, no. 3 (January 2006): 247–260.

Metzger, Michael. "Leviathan's Labors Lost, or: Who Works After the Subject?" *Millenium Film Journal* (Spring 2015): 38–48.

Moore, Jason W. "The Capitalocene, Part I: On the Nature and Origins of Our Ecological Crisis," *The Journal of Peasant Studies* (March 2017): 1–37.

Nicholls, Robert J. "Coastal Megacities and Climate Change." *GeoJournal 37*, no. 3 (1995): 369–379.

Nichols, Bill. *Representing Reality: Issues and Concepts in Documentary.* Bloomington: Indiana University Press, 1991.

Nichols, Bill. "Documentary Reenactment and the Fantasmatic Subject." *Critical Inquiry* 35, no.1 (Autumn 2008): 72–89.

Nornes, Abé Mark. *Cinema Babel: Translating Global Cinema.* Minneapolis: U of Minnesota P, 2007.

Nosal, Andrew P., Elizabeth A. Keenan, Philip A. Hastings, and Ayelet Gneezy. "The Effect of Background Music in Shark Documentaries on Viewers' Perceptions of Sharks." *PLoS ONE* 11, no. 8 (August 2016). https://journals.plos.org/plosone/article?id=10.1371/journal.pone.0159279.

O'Fait, Chris. "Kanopy: The Free Netflix Alternative Adds 100 Classic Paramount Titles—Exclusive." *Indiewire*, June 6, 2018. https://www.indiewire.com/2018/06/kanopy-free-netflix-alternative-adds-100-classic-paramount-movies-1201971739/.

Özen, Saadet. "'Balkanlar'ın İlk Sinemacıları' Mı?: Manaki Biraderler." *Toplumsal Tarih, no. 219* (2012): 60–67.

Özgüç, Agah. *Türk Filmleri Sözlüğü,* 3rd ed. Istanbul: Horizon International, 2012.

Peranson, Mark. "First You Get the Power, Then You Get the Money: Two Models of Film Festivals." *Cineaste 33*, no. 3 (2008): 37–43. Reprinted in *Dekalog 3: On Film Festivals,* edited by Richard Porton, 23-37. London: Wallflower, 2009.

Plantinga, Carl. "American Documentary in the 1980s." In *Hollywood under the Electronic Rainbow, 1980–1989,* edited by Stephen Prince, 370–387. Berkeley: University of California Press, 2002.

Rogers, Holly. "Introduction: Music, Sound and the Nonfiction Aesthetic." In *Music and Sound in Documentary Film,* edited by Holly Rogers, 1–19. New York: Routledge, 2015.

Rogers, Katherine M. *Cat.* London: Reaktion Books, 2006.

Rony, Fatimah Tobing. *The Third Eye: Race, Cinema, and Ethnographic Spectacle.* Durham, NC: Duke University Press, 1996.

Schnabel, Tom. "Kedi: A Sweet Film and Soundtrack for Istanbul's Constant Companions." https://www.kcrw.com/music/articles/kedi-a-sweet-film-and-soundtrack-for-istanbuls-constant-companions.

Shepard, Paul. *The Others: How Animals Made Us Human.* Washington DC/Covelo, CA: Island Press/Shearwater Books, 1996.

Simon, Alissa. "Turkish Helmer's Debut Doc 'Kedi' Tapped for U.S. Release." *Variety,* October 18, 2016. https://variety.com/2016/film/festivals/turkish-helmers-debut-doc-kedi-tapped-for-u-s-release-1201892894/.

Smith, Jeff. "Popular Songs and Comic Allusion in Contemporary Cinema." In *Soundtrack Available: Essays on Film and Popular Music*, edited by Pamela Robertson Wojcik and Arthur Knight, 407–430. Durham, NC: Duke University Press, 2001.

Smith, Jeff. *The Sounds of Commerce: Marketing Popular Film Music*. New York: Columbia University Press, 1998.

Spangler, Todd. "YouTube Acquires Turkish Street Cats Documentary Film 'Kedi' for YouTube Red." *Variety*, April 20, 2017. https://variety.com/2017/digital/news/youtube-red-kedi-turkish-street-cats-1202391313/.

Spicer, Daniel. *The Turkish Psychedelic Music Explosion: Anadolu Psych 1965-1980*. London: Repeater, 2017.

Swinton, Tilda. "The View from Here." *Sight & Sound 30*, no.4 (April 2020): 33.

Tong, Chris. "Ecocinema for All: Reassembling the Audience." *Interactions: Studies in Communication & Culture 4*, no. 2 (October 1, 2013): 113–128.

Toros, Hüseyin, Mohsen Abbasnia, Mustafa Sagdic, and Mete Tayanç. "Long-Term Variations of Temperature and Precipitation in the Megacity of Istanbul for the Development of Adaptation Strategies to Climate Change." *Advances in Meteorology 2017* (2017).

Tsing, Anna Lowenhaupt. *The Mushroom at the End of the World: On the Possibility of Life in Capitalist Ruins*. Princeton, NJ: Princeton University Press, 2015.

Tsing, Anna Lowenhaupt, Heather Anne Swanson, Elaine Gan, and Nils Bubandt. *Arts of Living on a Damaged Planet. Ghosts of the Anthropocene; Monsters of the Anthropocene*. Minneapolis: University of Minnesota Press, 2017.

Tunç, Aslı. "Girgir as a Sociological Phenomenon in Turkey: The Transformation of a Humor Magazine." *Humor 14*, no. 3 (2001): 243–254.

"Turkey's Failed Coup Attempt: All You Need to Know," 2017. https://www.aljazeera.com/news/2016/12/turkey-failed-coup-attempt-161217032345594.html.

"Turkey Sends Philanthropist Back to Prison despite European Ruling." *Al-Monitor*, 2020. https://www.al-monitor.com/pulse/originals/2020/01/turkish-court-osman-kavala-prison-defy-un-human-rights-court.html.

"Turkish Court Cases over 'insulting' the President up 30 Percent in 2018." *Middle East Eye*, 2019. https://www.middleeasteye.net/news/26000-people-investigated-insulting-erdogan-2018.

Tutui, Marian. *"Balkan Cinema versus Cinema of the Balkan Nations,"* http://aqshf.gov.al/uploads/2.___Manakia_Bros_Pioneers_of_Balkan_Cinema_Claimed_by_Six_Nations.pdf.

Tryon, Chuck. *On Demand Culture: Digital Delivery and the Future of Movies*. New Brunswick: Rutgers University Press, 2013.

Tzioumakis, Yannis. "'Independent,' 'Indie,' and 'Indiewood': Towards a Periodisation of Contemporary (post-1980) American Independent Cinema." In *American Independent Cinema*, edited by Geoff King, Claire Malloy, and Yannis Tzioumakis, 28–40. London: Routledge, 2012.

Uhlin, Graig. "On Street Cats and City Rats: Synanthropes and Cinematic Ecologies." *The Cine-Files*, no. 14 (Spring 2019). http://thecine-files.com/uhlin/.

Vallejo, Aida. "Documentary Filmmakers on the Circuit: A Festival Career from *A Czech Dream* to a *Czech Peace.*" In *Post-1990 Documentary: Reconfiguring Independence*, edited by Camille Deprez and Judith Pernin, 171–187. Edinburgh: Edinburgh University Press, 2015.

Vardan, Uğur. "Mumya Yine Firarda…." *Hürriyet*, June 10, 2017. https://www.hurriyet.com.tr/yazarlar/ugur-vardan/mumya-yine-firarda-40484488.

Vidal, John. "'Tip of the Iceberg': Is Our Destruction of Nature Responsible for Covid-19?" *The Guardian*, March 18, 2020. https://www.theguardian.com/environment/2020/mar/18/tip-of-the-iceberg-is-our-destruction-of-nature-responsible-for-covid-19-aoe.

Wang, Yiman. "*Kedi*: A Feline City Symphony." *Docalogue* (May 2018). https://docalogue.com/may-kedi/.

"Wave of Terror Attacks in Turkey Continue at a Steady Pace." *The New York Times*, June 28, 2016. https://www.nytimes.com/interactive/2016/06/28/world/middleeast/turkey-terror-attacks-bombings.html.

White, Jerry. "National Belonging." *New Review of Film and Television Studies 2*, no. 2 (2004): 211–232.

Whitten, Sarah. "Netflix's disappointing Oscar night has some questioning its film strategy." *CNBC.com*, February 16, 2020. https://www.cnbc.com/2020/02/14/oscars-2020-netflixs-disappointing-night-raises-questions-about-strategy.html.

Williams, John L. *America's Mistress: The Life and Times of Eartha Kitt*, London: Quercus, 2013.

Yalçınkaya, Turhan. "A Shift in the Tradition of Humour Magazines in Turkey: The Case of L-Manyak and Lombak." *Middle East Technical University*, 2006. https://etd.lib.metu.edu.tr/upload/12608118/index.pdf.

Yazar, Mahir, Dina Hestad, Diana Mangalagiu, Ali Kerem Saysel, Yuge Ma, and Thomas F. Thornton. "From Urban Sustainability Transformations to Green Gentrification: Urban Renewal in Gaziosmanpaşa, Istanbul." *Climatic Change*, August 1, 2019.

Zimmerman, Andrea Luka. "ERASURES: Being, Seen." *Erase* (Singapore: LASALLE College of the Arts) 8 (2019): 17–33.

# Filmography

*38* (Çayan Demirel, 2006)
*2016: Obama's America* (Dinesh D'Souza, John Sullivan, 2012)
*Abacus: Too Small to Jail* (Steve James, 2017)
*The Act of Killing* (Joshua Oppenheimer, 2012)
*Amélie* (Jean-Pierre Jeunet, 2001)
*An Inconvenient Sequel* (Bonni Cohen, Jon Shenk, 2017)
*An Inconvenient Truth* (Davis Guggenheim, 2006)
*Babies* (Thomas Balmès, 2010)
*Bakur* (*North*, Çayan Demirel and Ertuğrul Mavioğlu, 2015)
*Benim Çocuğum* (*My Child*, Can Candan, 2013)
*Bestiaire* (Denis Côté, 2012)
*Bombshell: The Hedy Lamarr Story* (Alexandra Dean, 2017)
*Born in China* (Lu Chuan, 2017)
*Brimstone and Glory* (Viktor Jakovleski, 2017)
*California Typewriter* (Doug Nichol, 2017)
*The Case of the Grinning Cat* (Chris Marker, 2004)
*The Cat Rescuers* (Rob Fruchtman and Steve Lawrence, 2018)
*Chasing Coral* (Jeff Orlowski, 2017)
*Chasing Trane: The John Coltrane Documentary* (John Scheinfeld, 2017)
*City of God* (Fernando Meirelles, Kátia Lund, 2002)
*Crossing the Bridge: The Sound of Istanbul* (Fatih Akın, 2005)
*Demolition of the Russian Monument in San Stefano* (Fuat Uzkınay, 1914)
*The Eagle Huntress* (Otto Bell, 2017)
*Etre et Avoir* (Nicolas Philibert, 2002)
*Faces Places* (Agnès Varda, JR, 2017)
*Fahrenheit 9/11* (Michael Moore, 2004)
*Fire at Sea* (Gianfraco Rosi, 2017)
*Get Out* (Jordan Peele, 2017)
*The Grin Without a Cat* (Chris Marker, 1977)
*Grizzly Man* (Werner Herzog, 2005)
*Hasret* (*Yearning*, Ben Hopkins, 2016)
*Hitit Güneşi* (*The Hittite Sun*, Sabahattin Eyuboglu and Mazhar Şevket İpşiroğlu, 1956)

*Homeland: Iraq Year Zero* (Abbas Fahdel, 2015)

*Honeyland* (Tamara Kotevska, Ljubomir Stefanov, 2019)

*Hoop Dreams* (Steve James, 1994)

*I Am Not Your Negro* (Raoul Peck, 2017)

*Icarus* (Bryan Fogel, 2017)

*İki Dil Bir Bavul* (*On the Way to School*, Özgür Doğan and Orhan Eskiköy, 2008)

*Innocence of Memories* (Grant Gee and Orhan Pamuk, 2016)

*Is Genesis History?* (Thomas Purifoy, 2017)

*Jackie* (Pablo Larrain, 2017)

*Jane* (Brett Morgen, 2017)

*Joan Didion: The Center Will Not Hold* (Griffin Dunne, 2017)

*Johnny Morris Takes a Ticket to Turkey* (BBC, 1960)

*Karl Marx City* (Michael Tucker and Petra Epperlein, 2017)

*Koyaanisqatsi* (Godfrey Reggio, 1983)

*Last Men in Aleppo* (Feras Fayyad, 2017)

*Leviathan* (Lucien Castaing-Taylor and Véréna Paravel, 2012)

*Manchester by the Sea* (Kenneth Lonergan, 2017)

*March of the Penguins* (Luc Jacquet, 2005)

*Nénette* (Nicolas Philbert, 2010)

*No Home Movie* (Chantal Akerman, 2017)

*Obit* (Vanessa Gould, 2017)

*Paris is Burning* (Jennie Livingston, 1990)

*Rat Film* (Theo Anthony, 2016)

*Roman J. Israel, Esq.* (Dan Gilroy, 2017)

*Step* (Amanda Lipitz, 2017)

*Strong Island* (Yance Ford, 2017)

*The Summit* (Nick Ryan, 2013)

*Sweetgrass* (Lucien Castaing-Taylor, 2009)

*Taskafa: Stories of the Street* (Andrea Luka Zimmerman, 2013)

*The Thin Blue Line* (Errol Morris, 1988)

*Türk İnkılabında Terakki Hamleleri* (*The Leaps of Progress in Turkish Reforms*, Esfir Schub, 1937)

*Türkiye'nin Kalbi Ankara* (*Ankara, Heart of Turkey*, Sergei Yutkevitch and Lev Oscarovich Arnstam, 1934)

*Turkish Chronicles* (Maurice Pialat, 1963–64)

*The Visit of Sultan Mehmet V to Bitola and Thessaloniki* (Yanaki and Milton Manaki, 1905)

*Yeryüzü Aşkın Yüzü Oluncaya Dek* (*Love Will Change the Earth*, Reyan Tuvi, 2014)

# Contributor Biographies

**Melis Behlil** is an Associate Professor of Cinema Studies and Chair of Radio, Television and Cinema Department at Kadir Has University in Istanbul, Turkey. She has been a visiting scholar at Massachusetts Institute of Technology and a Research Associate at Stockholm University. In addition to teaching and other academic duties, she writes film reviews for various publications, co-hosts a weekly radio show, and is a member of the Turkish Film Critics Association, for which she served as president in 2014-15.

**Chris Cagle** is Associate Professor of Film and Media Arts at Temple University. His recent book is *Sociology on Film: Postwar Hollywood's Prestige Commodity* (Rutgers University Press), an examination of the Hollywood social problem film. He has published in *Cinema Journal*, *Screen*, *Film Criticism*, and *Quarterly Review of Film and Video* and in a number of edited volumes, including *Cinematography* (Rutgers University Press) and *Vocal Projections: Voices in Documentary* (Bloomsbury). He is working on a book on film-festival documentary aesthetics and politics.

**Paul N. Reinsch** is Associate Professor of Practice – Cinema in the School of Theatre and Dance at Texas Tech University. He is the author of *An Annotated Bibliography of Shirley Jackson* (2001) and an editor of *The Soundtrack Album: Listening to Media* (2020) and *Python beyond Python: Critical Engagements with Culture* (2017). His work has appeared in edited collections, and journals such as *Music and the Moving Image*, *Spectrum: A Journal on Black Men*, *Quarterly Review of Film and Video* and *Flow*.

**Benjamin Schultz-Figueroa** is Assistant Professor in Film Studies at Seattle University. He earned his PhD in Film and Digital Media from

University of California Santa Cruz and his MA in Media Studies from The New School. His research focuses on the history of scientific filmmaking, nontheatrical film, and animal representations on film. His published works include "Celluloid Specimens: Animal Origins for the Moving Image," in *Viscera, Skin, and Physical Form: Corporeality and Early Cinema* and "From Cage to Classroom: Animal Testing and Behaviorist Educational Film" in *Film History* (Winter 2019). His book *The Celluloid Specimen: Moving Image Research into Animal Life* is due to be published by UC Press in 2022.

**Ceyda Torun** is the director/producer of *Kedi*, her first feature documentary. Born in Istanbul, she lived in Amman, Jordan and New York before studying anthropology at Boston University. She worked with director Reha Erdem in Istanbul and producer Chris Auty in London before returning to the United States, where she co-founded Termite Films with cinematographer Charlie Wuppermann.

**Yiman Wang** is Professor of Film & Digital Media at University of California, Santa Cruz. She is the author of *Remaking Chinese Cinema: Through the Prism of Shanghai, Hong Kong and Hollywood* (Honolulu, HI: University of Hawaii Press, 2013) and guest editor of the Asian Media special issue of *Feminist Media Histories* (2019). She has published numerous articles in journals and edited volumes. She is currently completing a monograph on Anna May Wong, the best-known early 20th century Chinese-American screen-stage performer.

# Index

112    *Index*

For Product Safety Concerns and Information please contact our EU
representative GPSR@taylorandfrancis.com
Taylor & Francis Verlag GmbH, Kaufingerstraße 24, 80331 München, Germany